This book is dedicated to my grandfather, John Homer Woolsey, M.D. for his preservation of a personal and historical insight into the life of a young man facing a great challenge during a period of turmoil. Dr Woolsey was a surgeon during WWI and knew the hardship of men during times of conflict. He served in France as a young surgeon on the frontline. During a tearful conversation with my grandfather, he told me my father was not the same man who left to go to war. War takes its toll on everyone.

It is also dedicated to my father, "Jack" Woolsey and my father's fellow crewmen and the ancillary ground crews that kept the Liberators flying and safe.

Finally to my daughter Shelley Herbert, a WWII history student, who knew the significance of the missions that my father flew in relation to the greater war effort, and to my step-son, Duncan Herbert, a Hornet pilot in the Australian Air Force, who talked to my father at length about his experiences and how they related to modern day warfare.

Copyright © Elizabeth Woolsey Herbert 2015

ISBN 978-0-994-29720-4 (paperback)
    978-0-994-29721-1 (ebook)

Jack's War

Letters from an American WWII

Navigator

Edited by Elizabeth Woolsey Herbert, DVM

Introduction

John Homer Woolsey (Jack) was born on July 14, 1923 in San Francisco. He moved to Woodland California when he was ten and he attended Woodland High School.

Jack's college studies at U.C. Berkeley were interrupted when America was brought into the war following Pearl Harbor in December 1941. He enlisted in the Army Air Corps and on April 2, 1943, at the age of nineteen Jack left his family, his devoted dog, Toots, and his horses Koli and Lady.

He flew 35 missions over Germany as a Liberator navigatormand then returned stateside to begin pilot training when the war ended. He was discharged in October 1945.

Jack wrote to his family on most Sundays. Each letter was preserved in an album by his father. These letters describe his initiation into army life, his basic and navigational training at various camps and reflect his thoughts and personal experiences along the way. Like many men away from home, he loved his packages of food and news from his hometown and family.

Jack did not speak of these events until very late in life when he reminisced with his step-grandson, a pilot in the Royal Australian Air Force. That album of 140 weekly letters and another album that contained his original maps and mission notes were retrieved from the closet where they had remained for decades until his death in 2011.

These documents and letters are a valuable historical source for both his family and other families who may have also had fathers, grandfathers and uncles who serve in the Army Air Corps during WWII. They also provide historians with an incredible source of archival information regarding the missions that were flown over Germany during the war.

Jack's War – Letters to home from an American WWII Navigator

Jack's War

Part 1

Chapter 1 Journey to Basic tralning in Texas

Chapter 2 Sheppard Field Wichita Falls, Texas

Chapter 3 Texas Technical College Lubbock Texas

Chapter 4 Classification Center Santa Ana

Chapter 5 Ellington Field Texas Navigation School

Chapter 6 Graduation from Ellington Navigation School

Chapter 7 Lincoln Air Force Base

Chapter 8 Gowan Field Boise, Idaho 212th Combat Crew Training School

Chapter 9 Going to War

Chapter 10 The E.T. O.

Chapter 11 Finishing Up

Chapter 12 The War is Over

Part 2

Mission Statements and Maps in the E.T.O

Part 1

The Letters

Chapter 1

Journey to Basic Training in Texas

April 2nd, 1943 Leaving for Basic Training

1 – April 2nd, 1943 (on the train)

Dear Mother and Dad,

Had a marvellous trip so far. The Pine forests on way up to the summit with all the snow around them. Had a wonderful view of Donner Lake and the river coming out from there. Ate dinner (big one despite grievous advice as I am from Missouri) thru the pass into Reno Nevada. The river looked inviting for trout fishing and the high rocky crags really made it beautiful. The Nevada stockmen are beginning to turn their stock out in the meadows but the feed is way behind California time. I am now sitting in the Reno station waiting to pull out. Will try to get this off. Going to have a big poker game tonight so don't worry.

Jack

2 – April 3rd, 1943 (On the train from Reno to Ogden)

Dear Mother and Dad,

Spent an uneventful but restful night. Slept like a log. I awoke as we were crossing the salt beds and I ate breakfast as we travelled on the trestle over the Great Salt Lake. We are just about to pull into Ogden where we set our watches an hour ahead. I am sure having a good time. Haven't done much reading as yet as the country is absorbing my interest.

Jack

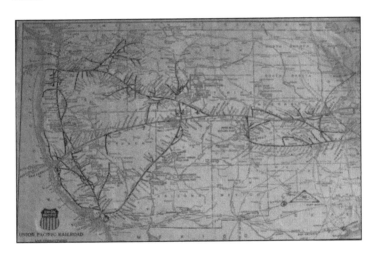

Map from California to Texas

3 – April 4th, 1943 Postcard

Denver

Dear Mother and Dad,

There is no meat shortage in Denver. Just had four slices of bacon on a 35 ¢ breakfast. Still enjoying the trip and the country. It is pretty desolate along the lower border of Wyoming, but very interesting to me. The feed looks terrible but the cattle seem to be well. In one bunch of cattle I saw an elk which seemed to have strayed down from the mountains. There are quite a few horses, but from the train they look like a mix of Shetland pony and work horses. The snow is just melting and rivers swift and brown. In one place I saw ice and snow right in the river. Well see you later. I am off to view Denver.

Jack

4 – April 4th, 1943 Postcard

Denver

Dear folks

Just about ready to pull out for Wichita. Saw Union Stockyards (immense), City Park, zoo, civic center, and capital buildings. Having wonderful weather here. Say hello to Toots.

Jack

Jack's War – Letters to home from an American WWII Navigator

Chapter 2

Sheppard Field Wichita Falls, Texas

5 – April 6th, 1943

Sheppard Field Texas Wichita Falls Texas

Dear Mother and Dad,

I'll have to write on this old German paper being as we are in a hurry. Had another good ride down from Denver. Really enjoyed the country and saw Pikes Peak. The train was late so didn't arrive in Wichita Falls until 2:20 A.M. We(about 107 boys) were met there by two sergeants. We were taken to the Field by 3 buses. For the rest of the morning we just stood and waited. Sheppard Field is quite a bit like Mather and didn't seem too bad to me. When we marched to lunch we were greeted by shouts "You'll be sorry" and "Where are you from?"

There are thousands here and not too many are Air Corps cadets. Some are pretty ignorant looking and others pretty intelligent. After lunch we had a small physical. I walked between two men and they gave me a shot in each arm so fast I couldn't tell them anything so I just didn't say anything____. Just learned how to make a bed the army way and also just had dinner. You have plenty to eat, and it isn't bad in my estimation.

One certainly hears a great difference of opinions. Most say this is the hottest worst hell hole in Texas. Some say they have been waiting 6-7 months to go to college. As far as I can see it, won't be half as bad as my first days at Standard Oil, and it looks like it will be a lot of fun. I think we will stay here six weeks for basic training and take tests which determine the length of our stay in some Southwestern college. Oh yes we were being shipped over to

Guadalcanal any day now. Not sure this is my right address but it should reach me.

Jack

6 – April 7th, 1943
Sheppard Field
Wichita Falls Texas
Dear Mother and Dad,

There doesn't seem like anything else to do but write letters or other it isn't as much work as it used to be. I would first like you to send me some hangers (10 of them). Also if you want me to send my letters via airmail (this seems to be the way because the other takes pretty long) you better send me some more air mail envelopes.

We were issued our G.I. clothes (dad will explain that mother) and I am sending my clothes home C.O.D. We had a lot of talks today on army customs and ways of doing things. When we were all sitting around listening to the Corporal he asked us to raise our hands if we had gone to college. I shot my hand in the air thinking I was one of the privileged few. Well the Corporal spotted me and called me to the front and said "If you're just out of college I guess you can read so read a couple of chapters out of this Army handbook to the rest of the Cadets." Sometimes I think that the non-commissioned officers don't appreciate college men.

I think at the end of this week we start marching and learning the manual of arms. This is going to be pretty dull as I had this in college R.O.T. C. They call the drill field the "cow pasture" because it is so dusty. They have a quaint saying about Sheppard Field; they say that S.F. is only on the ground when it is raining, the rest of the time it is up in the air. This is because it is so windy most of the time. 9:00 P. M. - 5:00 A.M. well what do you know it is

Jack's War – Letters to home from an American WWII Navigator

raining this morning. I guess we will be on what they call a rainy day schedule. This probably means lectures or training films.

I sure would like to have the democrat sent down here is possible. Well I have to sweep and mop around the bunks so I better close.

Jack

7 – April 11th, 1943
Sunday 3:30 pm
Sheppard Field
Wichita Falls, Texas
Dear Mother and Dad,

I'll start on my third letter to though none of yours have reached me as yet. We had our second typhoid shots yesterday and I think it made me kind of sick and my arm sore but I am sure I will be alright Monday. Sunday is our day of and I have been resting on my bed all day.

A very strange thing happened 5 minutes ago. We were all called out of our barracks and massed around a small platform where we were told to take in all our mops and brooms and loose articles around the barracks that there might be a Tornado right over Sheppard Field. Now actually the chances are 100 to one but we have to take precautions anyway they expect it at 5:00 PM if it is coming so I will wait with the letter and let you know whether it did.

We haven't done much but drill although we did have a test the other morning at 5:00 A.M. to determine our length of stay in college if we if we get to go to college. I am still worried about that physical we have to take. There are a large number of cadet who wash out who come back here and they say they are very tough so you can see we do nothing but worry most of the time. This next week we will really start working hard. Most men and boys around here don't like it but the bunch we're in haven't seen anything too bad except dust.

I guess I told you I needed about 10 hangers and I sure would appreciate it if you could send the Democrat once in a while. We are now waiting for the Tornado____

Well the all clear has been sounded and nothing happened, I guess it veered off. Say hello to Toots for me.

Jack

8 – April 16th, 1943 Friday
Sheppard Field
    Dear Mother and Dad,

I can't remember what I told you in my first letter so first I'll answer some of your questions.

As to Address

A.S.N. =assigned serial number

308 Sr Sqd =Service Squadron

Bks 625 =Barracks 625

B. T. C. =Basic Training Center

Your letters really come thru fast. Received the one you mailed on the 13th on the 16th which is very good.

I am certainly surprised at Captain Woolsey's lack of knowledge. G.I. is simply Government Issue. Your clothes, coffee, food, shoes anything you receive in the army is G. I. We had a G.I. party just this afternoon. The govt. provided the soap and water and brushes, and we scrubbed the barracks.

Jack's War – Letters to home from an American WWII Navigator

I have two different uniforms, my O. D. or olive drab with the coat and my khakis (a light tan shirt with pants to match). I guess I told you the army has two sizes, too small and too large. I received size too large pants and too small shirt, but I can have them tailored. They didn't have shoes to fit about 15 of us, so just yesterday we were ordered to our barracks and told not to march or run until we received our army shoes. The supply Sargent said it would take two weeks for them to arrive. I don't know whether we will have to sit around or not. Most of the boys don't like the afternoon recreation, and we all kick about it, but personally I kind of like it. This obstacle course is really pretty tough and a lot of the boys don't get through the whole run. I found I was in better shape that I thought I was.

We sleep in bunks and the boy below comes from Boise, Idaho and his name is Harry Tritchman. We get along very well together. In fact I think I was pretty lucky. Lots of the boys have not attended college, but he had two years and is definitely a high type. The boys next to us are good fellows also. One is from Utah and the other from Montana. The one from Utah is Al Carter, and his father is a Captain in the Engineer Corp and stationed at Tracy California. The one from Montana is named Johnny O'Leary. He is married and has a 3 month old son, but you would never know it except he spent $29 talking to his wife on the phone.

Oh yes I took out a ten thousand dollar life insurance yesterday. I automatically get this free when and if I get to pre-flight. Remember everything depends on this upcoming physical.

I saw by the results of the track meet the other day that I might have done pretty well in the javelin. That's when I miss college. Well it's time to read the Saturday Evening Post so I'll close. Oh yes I would enjoy any eats sent here and also am looking forward to seeing the Democrat.

Jack

P.S. I hope you're not showing these letters to everybody that comes over.

9–Wednesday night 21 April 1943
Sheppard Field Texas

Dear Mother and Dad

Received hangers and nuts and also your first letter that you wrote and mailed on April the 8th. We certainly enjoyed the nuts and anything else along that line would also be appreciated.

We have been doing about the same thing as described in the last letter except for an actual use of our gas masks. This practical demonstration was given to us for two purposes. 1. To gain confidence in our masks 2. To learn how to enter a gas aid station.

We all lined up outside this gas chamber and put on our masks. We then entered in a certain procedure which is important on the battle field because the idea out there is not to let any gas in. You understand in our case the gas was in the building, but the procedure of entering is the same. We go in 3 at a time after you hear 2 knocks, then close outside door. Then we go in second door to the chamber filled with gas. The first time you have your mask on and it is hard to believe there is tear gas in there. Before they let you out they make you take your mask off. Your eyes begin to sting and water and you think you will never get out alive but you do. It was after this that I gave my gas mask its first affectionate look. We then lined up again and entered with gas mask off and instructions to put them on as fast as you can. When you first hit the gas you couldn't open your eyes but luckily and due to practice I put mine on in second time. It certainly was a kick to stand there and watch the others come in and fumble around with huge tears in there (sic) eyes. Needless to say I love my little gas mask like a brother now.

Today we started preliminary rifle marksmanship. I had already had this in college so it was very easy. We did not shoot the guns but learned the different positions and how to sight. They also took about a test tube full of blood for the Khan test (a test for syphilis). Lots of the boys are getting sick over this typhoid and small pox shots, but as far I am feeling fine and raring to go. We are still without G.I. shoes and they are keeping us out of the afternoon recreation. This is okay but I kind of miss the exercise.

I imagine we are about to ready to take one of these physicals and after that if we pass we will be ready to "ship" out for college. I think I am going to get that money back for the extra train berth. Well anyway I stood in line for 2 hours and signed my name to on a piece of paper. They have a saying here which is not very hard to believe. "There are two ways to get a job done The "right" way and the "Army way".

I guess I haven't told you about the singing. We can sing while we are marching and we have several good songs. It sounds pretty good to me but sometimes your (sic) too tired to sing. This is after marching a long time. They do have one song at this time which goes to the tune of Hinkey, Dinkey Parley Vouz (Dad will sing this mother).

Sing { "They say this is an aerial war Parley Vouz

       repeat

       They say this is an aerial war, so what the hell are we marching for

     Hinkey dinkey Parley Vouz.

I have received a letter from Aunt Grace and Aunt Katherine. Aunt Katherine says she going to Arizona.

Well this is about all the news of late so I guess I'LL close.

Jack

Easter 1943

This day brings memories of home

And every memory

Jack's War – Letters to home from an American WWII Navigator

Prompts worlds of Easter wishes

All as loving as can be

Wishes that this day will bring

True Easter joys to you

And that the year ahead will bring you

Many blessings, too.

Jack

10 – April 25th, 1943 Sunday
Sheppard Field
　　　Dear Mother and Dad,

　　　Well I have finally received all your letters. I just received Dad's first letter yesterday. You see they did not have the correct address. I have not received the "brownies" yet but don't worry it always takes packages longer.

　　　We had our physical Thursday morning and I passed, I think. This is not the physical I was expecting. This is what they call the #63. We are now ready to ship out to some college and it wouldn't surprise me if we left within the next two weeks. It is after college that we go to what they call pre-flight and it is there that we get the #64 physical which is the toughest in the army. Dad do you remember that day we went over to the clinic and you sat me in in that eye test chair. Well when I went over there to have my eyes tested by Dr Grey he gave me a lot of things that we have to do for the #64, such as two lines crossing+ and a dot that splits when so close and a few other things. I wish you would consult him and see if there are not some eye exercises I could do to improve my eyes. Also my blood pressure was exceedingly high 134 and my pulse was 93. Our blood pressure has to be under 134 to pass the next

18

physical (#64). Is there any way to bring these down. Are not there some drugs you can take just before that quiet you down and bring your blood pressure down? **Please** see about this because it is very important to me that I pass the next physical even if it is two or three more months off.

We have not done much this last week. We did have preliminary marksmanship with a rifle but I had this and more in R.O.T.C. We also had a lecture on how to walk guard and how to challenge people. I enjoyed the lecture, especially some of the incidents they told us about that happened here.

That article you sent me was very interesting and I will look into that the day I am washed out, if I am. I hope lady has had her colt by now and is getting along fine. Say hello to Toots. Oh yes, I am not receiving the Democrat, are you sure you gave them the right address. Thanks for the Easter card.

Jack

11 – April 29th, 1943
Sheppard Field, Texas
Dear Mother and Dad,

I don't know what's the matter with the mail service, but you must not be getting my letters. I received the brownies last Tuesday and they were good. Needless to say we finished them that very day. Thank you very much we sure do appreciate them. Don't think we are starving or we don't have the same advantages as you civilians. The food is simple but you learn to like it. We get all the ice cream we want. One pint for 10 ¢. I have had a chocolate Sundae practically every day. We can buy all the candy we want but we sure do like cookies.

Has any propaganda reached you as to the modernized kitchens for our army and the small amount of work for the K.P.?

Jack's War – Letters to home from an American WWII Navigator

Well we do have modernized kitchens but the other statement is false as false can be. The other day a man in our barracks had to be relieved on K.P. as he had an appointment. There were four men left and I was one of them. Out came the dice (dice decide everything in the army) and I lost. I arrived there just as they began cleaning out the garbage cans (30 of them). We were told to scrub them out. We did. Along came an inspector and said scrub them again. We did. Another inspector came by and said "they're still dirty" clean them again. We did. It was then time for lunch so we didn't get to clean them again. The boys eat on tin plates. I stood at the end of a machine which turned out these dirty plates clean. I then carried them back to where the boys take them to start down the chow line. I started at 11:00 am and didn't stop once until 1:00P.M. If I did stop this machine would pile up the plates. I carried 2000 of them and thought sure I would get a rest but no. I was sent out to scrub the garbage cans and scrub out the mess hall floor. I had to attend a meeting and so was relieved.

Well I guess you get the idea that no matter how mechanized and modernized army kitchens become, K.P. duty is still plain hell.

Had a very interesting day yesterday. We learned how to fight with bayonets. This is about the first practical training we have had and everyone worked hard on it. First you make a long thrust, then you step forward and you pull it out (of the Jap). This has to be done just right or he will fall, on you. You then give him a short thrust and remove it again. By this time he is about finished so you jab him in the throat twice. This may be a bit gory but that is just the way they gave it to us.

I'm glad to hear that Koli is looking fine and is being well taken care of. I imagine Lady has had her colt by now. Be sure and breed her back to Final Appeal if you think you can manage it. Oh yes, we went in town the other night. Nothing much there but a big

U.S.O. About that Commonwealth Blank this is probably for men in California who have been in the service for more than a year. I just can't answer but these of these questions and will have to go to bed.

Jack

12 – May 1st, 1943
Sheppard Field Texas
Dear Mother and Dad,

Well we are finally going to college. We were awakened at 5:30 A.M. and were told that we were all on shipping orders. That means we are going to college and not North Africa or England. We certainly are happy to get out of here on account of the dust. Everyone hopes to go as far north as possible.

My personal opinion is that we will go to some Southwest college as Texas A&M or Oklahoma. We never know until we get there. Had a very eventful day Saturday. I arose at 3:30 A.M. and stumbled over to the mess hall No. 9. I was immediately put to work. Yes, you guessed it, my second day of K.P. This rarely happens (two days of K.P. in the same week) so you can see I was highly honoured. We worked until 7:00 P.M. only sitting down for our meals. This time I worked right in the mess hall itself in fact. I dished out the salad and dressing as the boys came by. After every meal we had to sweep the whole place out and then scrub the floor in a military fashion. Mother aren't you glad you never made me do that at home. Think how uninteresting it would have made it here for me.

Went to town last night to the local U.S. O. They were having "Michigan Night". The building was loaded with soldiers as was the town. There really wasn't much to do so we went home. Keep writing to my old address until I send you my new one.

Jack

Jack's War – Letters to home from an American WWII Navigator

Chapter 3

Texas Technical College

Lubbock Texas

13 – May 4th, 1943

Texas Tech College,

Lubbock, Texas

Dear Mother and Dad,

I have just completed 24 hours at my new Post and it certainly is a change from Sheppard Field. It is the Texas Technological College (Texas Tech) located in Lubbock, Texas. We left Sheppard by train on Monday morning at 10:00 A.M. and arrived at Lubbock at 5:30 P.M. We came by way of Childress and then south to Lubbock. I thought it was a very interesting trip. The first 100 miles was like all the country around Sheppard, but after this we came on some real rough county and a few rocky hills. I think this is where the word "gulch" and "arroyo" came into being. They would appear in the ground for no reason with no outlet or beginning to them. I didn't see any good size trees all the way. The wind and the dust followed us all the way over, but it isn't going to be as bothersome now. We were brought to the campus (250 boys) in army trucks. It looks a little like Stanford without the eucalyptus trees. We were then marched in a boy's dormitory which was built in 1938. It is made of brick and is a really nice place as I've ever seen. It is three stories high and we have four to a room. We have two double bunks, large table, two closets, a wash basin and one dresser with a drawer to each man. We went down to dinner and had one of the best meals we have had since coming to the army. The school does the cooking and they really do a good job of it.

There are only about ten commissioned officers here so they make the cadets who have been here for three months student officers. They do all the drill instructing and really get good practice at being an officer. I suppose they are trying to make this place just like West point. The student officers come in your room and you snap to attention. They act as if they are generals or commanders. This is for our own good but it is very different from Sheppard. One fellow put his elbow on the able and they made him sit on the edge of a chair, look straight ahead and eat a square meal. I think they haze us for a while until we get on the beam, and then the will lay off. The one satisfaction is that in a certain time we will become officers ourselves.

We arise at 5:45 and start school at 7:30 and go to school till 12:30. We are then off till 2:00 then we drill and have athletics till 5:0 P.M. We haven't actually started yet but this will be our schedule. We filled out forms today putting down our college work so they can put us in flights. We are off at 6:30 till 8::30, then we study till 10:00 lights off at 10:15. I think this place will be pretty good after we get used to it.

I forgot to tell Dad, I met up with a fellow who tried out for the "Seals" when Nick Samborsky did. He was in our 308th training group composed of two thousand men. He played on their softball team and asked me to come down and play. The night I went down the 308th pitcher didn't show up so I pitched for them. The game ended in a tie 4 to 4. We should have won but the first baseman made an error and let the tying run in.

I never did get the Democrat. I sure would like to see it once in a while. I hope they send those cookies over here and your letters. Well, send me some pictures of the colt and take good care of Toots and Koli.

Jack

Jack's War – Letters to home from an American WWII Navigator

14 – May 8th, 1943 Saturday Night
Texas Tech College,
Lubbock, Texas
     Dear Mother and Dad,

     I'll settle that return address right now→ Army Air Force, Air Crew Detachment. Two hundred fifty of us boys were sent from Sheppard and we are squadron H. We are divided into thirty nine academic sections through a test we took at Sheppard and through our college work. Sections contain about thirty six boys and section thirty nine happens to be the top section of the whole bunch. I am telling you this so please don't tell anybody that your son is one of the smartest boys at Texas Tech. It is only because I went to college that I am in this section.

     We have changed our barracks in the last few days and we now go to school in the afternoon from one to six P.M. which is mighty long. Each period is 1:15 long. We have our P.E. and marching in the morning. The dormitory we are now living in is just as good as the last one and I can't get over the food. I feel really sorry for civilians. We always have meat twice a day and usually bacon in the morning.

     We practically have no time off now and are on the go from 6:00 A.M. to 10:30 P.M. We have plenty of homework which we are supposed to do between 7:30 and 10:15 but the army usually has something else in mind for us like marching, so we always cram at the last minute. They stress physics and math mostly, but we do have English (Public Speaking), History and Geography. Our History teacher is the Pastor of the local Lutheran Church and advocates early marriage so you can see he is quite a fellow.

     This place is really okay and I think I will like it in spite of the strict regulations. We will either stay here or go to school for four months and fly for one month or stay here for about 2 ½ months and then go to pre-flight.

    I guess you are wondering why I haven't sent any money home. Well I received only $28 to date. I have spent quite a bit for little things. Here is a copy of the insurance. I went to town tonight and had my picture taken for 25¢ as you can see the background is strictly California I will call Sunday nite unless I hear from you. I still am not receiving the Democrat. Well, I'll write again when I have time.

Jack early days

Jack

    P.S. I am sorry I forgot Mother's day, but I didn't remember it till today. Oh yes, if you see Uncle Leon tell him I received his money order and will write him again soon.

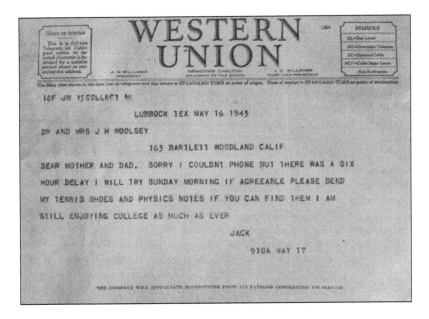

1943 Lubbock Texas

15 – May 19th, 1943 Tuesday
2030 Air corps Time 8:30 P.M.
Texas Tech College,
Lubbock, Texas

Dear Mother and Dad,

Sorry I didn't call but the operator said there would be a six hour delay and that would have made it around midnight. I will call early Sunday Morning about 7:00 A.M. your time because they say calls go through better.

Well we are really into the school work now and even though I have had this same work before they keep us plenty busy. I wish you would send me my navigations book and my meteorology book and also a little red book full of tables. There isn't anything new that happens here, every day is the same so consequently there is nothing to say.

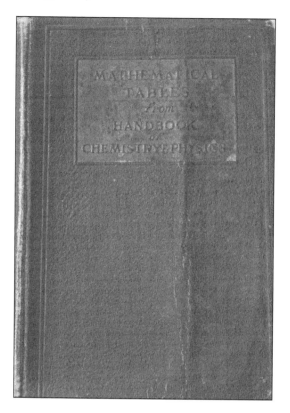

Jack's tables book used by his daughters during high school and university (pre calculators)

How is the new colt? I don't think there is a better name than Maybe.

Oh yes, the Democrat does not come! I don't know what's the matter with them, but why don't you phone Jay and give him my address and tell him to send it to me. It seems so simple, and I don't see how they keep bungling the works. Well I have to start studying so I'll close.

Jack

Jack's War – Letters to home from an American WWII Navigator

May 23rd, 1943

Note from Jack's father;

Jack called us by phone at 6:50 am. His voice was entirely natural. He was at a phone close to his room. He sounded happy and enthusiastic and had interesting plans for the day- a ride in a bomber plane or a glider. It was indeed a thrill to Beth and me to hear his voice and feel close to him.

16 – May 29th, 1943 Thursday
Texas Tech College,
Lubbock, Texas
Dear Mother and Dad,

Well I guess this letter is long overdue but as time goes on school get harder and we have less time to ourselves. Also there is a lack of news. We do practically the same thing every day.

Speaking of my roommates, do you remember the letter I sent you from Sheppard telling of my friend from Utah (Alan Carter) whose father was an engineer stationed at Tracey? Well he came here with me and is in the same section as I and we spend our weekends together. He received a letter from his father in which his father speaks of having dinner with Major Peden who knew a Jack Woolsey at Lubbock Texas. Quite a coincidence.

I again have some good roommates; the one who sleeps over me is Linn Wilson from Ft. Worth Texas. He is our Flight leader and does a very good job of it. One across the room is Bob Aidem who comes from Minnesota but has worked in California for the last few years. The other is Floyd Anderson from Springville Utah. He is a Mormon as are a great number of the boys in our group. I went to church with them one Sunday just to see what it was like. There is one other man here by the name of John Freeman who lived in

Ukiah and went to the University of California. He knows Humboldt County very well, and we have a lot of fun talking about it.

So far in school I have done pretty well, but this is only because it is repetition. As to postcards of the school, they don't have any and for a picture of myself; I haven't a camera and film is very scarce which makes it pretty hard to get them. I would like a ring very much and will send you my ring size also I will be looking forward to a picture of Koli.

Jack

17 – May 30th, 1943 Sunday
Texas Tech College,
Lubbock, Texas
Dear Mother and Dad,

I have received everything you have sent so far books, papers, Alpha Delta Phi and etc. Yes Texas Tech has a football team. I think they used to come up to San Francisco early in the season and play one of the teams up there. Their athletic staff has stayed on and are handling our physical training program, and I might add they are really putting us in condition. As to Lubbock being a cattle town, I don't know. We hardly have time to find out things of interest like that. It might be interesting to know that this town is 300 feet high and the weather up till now has been grand but now we are having a hot spell which makes it plenty uncomfortable in class.

I am sorry to hear about Charlie but I will be interested to hear what the Air Corps is going to do with him.

I still don't have anything new to tell you so I will elaborate on our Physical Training Program.

It lasts about an hour and a quarter. Every day we go out to the field in squadrons of three Flights each consisting of forty men

Jack's War – Letters to home from an American WWII Navigator

in other words a squadron consists of one hundred and twenty men. We do exercises for about twenty five minutes straight which really tires one out. We then play games for the remaining time. Every six weeks we take a physical test consisting one for building up our endurance, chinning on a bar, coming to a sitting position from lying flat on your back and running a 300 yard race. We are given points for each event, and if we do not show improvement we have been warned that we are liable for "washout". Friday is the big day for this is the day for building our endurance and you get out of it just what you put into it. It consists of a mile and a quarter cross country course finishing up on the obstacle course and then trying to sprint down a straight away.

We ran it; that is the whole squadron did for the first time this last Friday and it was really some race all one hundred and twenty of us.

I will show you a diagram of the course. We start in the football field on the track and finish up there too. When we started, I took the lead until twenty of us pulled away from the other one hundred. I was pretty winded when we reached the back stretch and three men passed me going like mad. They didn't get too far ahead and I was only about twenty yards behind when we reached the obstacle course. You can imagine trying to jump over hurdles and crouch under boards after running a mile. Much to my surprise when we reached the stadium I had gained on these men in front of me. We started down that last hundred yards with two men in front of me and blowing like wind broken horses. When we were about seventy five yards from the finish I passed the first one and was on the heels of the second one. We raced neck and neck for about thirty yards and then he just couldn't run so I won with about fifteen yards to spare.

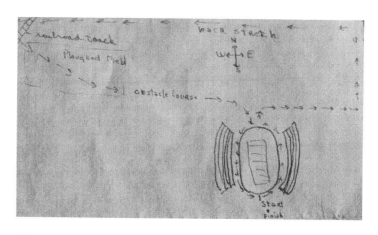

The running course

I think this amazed me more than anyone else for I doubted I would be able to run the whole distance without stopping. The average time the coaches told us was 10 minutes. My time was 7:47. This wasn't the record but it was a very good time the coaches said. Some fellow from Nebraska (a miler) set the record about 2 months ago. Two of those men I beat ran the 880 in high school and in college and wanted to know what college I run for.

This morning we went out to the airport and spent all morning talking to the cadets who were flying. They were very encouraging, and told us all about what was to come. Next Sunday we are going out to fly, we hope. Well I have to start studying.

Jack

P.S. Only received two Democrats last week. When addressed they come here but how often do they send them.

18 – May 30th, 1943 Sunday Night
Texas Tech Lubbock Texas
    Dear Dad.

Well it is the day before your birthday and I just found out that you can't send birthday congratulations from here in the form

Jack's War – Letters to home from an American WWII Navigator

of a night letter or a telegram. I don't know what you want or whether I could get it for you in Texas. So this letter will have to do until later. Being that all the news is in the other letter I will wish you a happy birthday and close.

Jack

19 – June 6th, 1943 Sunday
Texas Tech College,
Lubbock, Texas
        Dear Mother and Dad,

        Well here it is Sunday again and I have had a very quiet week. They have changed our schedule so we have morning classes and afternoon both. The classes only last an hour long. It has been very hot and sultry and we just sit in the classes and drip with perspiration. Our squadron has been on guard detail this week. I was senior officer of the guard one night, and was on duty from 1 A.M. to 6 A. M. and all I had to do was to go out every two hours and check the guard. The next time I walked a post from 7 P.M. to 9 P.M. and 1 A.M. to 3 A.M. The first time, a cloud storm blew up, and I have never seen it rain so hard, and the wind almost blew me over.

        You can send the license plates to the Jim Power at the A.D. P. house. Here is some money that I have left over from my pay check. You can do what you want with War Bonds or etc. (car for Jane if it would help).

        Maybe you could send me our old camera with some film to go with it because it is impossible to get films down here.

I am looking forward to seeing the pictures. In fact, I can't wait. How about sending that picture of Toots on my dresser. I think I would enjoy looking at her when I get up in the morning.

Received the cookie and they certainly were good. What do you want me to do with the tins?

Say Major Peden is coming down here is he? Did Stan Daly break his leg again?

The Democrat is being sent to Sheppard Field regularly now. Sometimes I wonder if the person who addresses them graduated from grammar school.

Well, we have a big Physics test tomorrow and being that I am gunning to be a navigator I will have to close and study.

Jack

P.S. There should be $45 in here if there isn't, next time I'll send a money order but nobody does around here.

20 – June 13th, 1943 Sunday
Texas Tech College,
Lubbock, Texas
Dear Mother and Dad,

I'll just answer a few questions first. Yes, I pay for the insurance until I start flying then the army does. The Democrat is coming regularly now------ straight from Sheppard Field. Your stationary is very fine and I think I can take it for two years. Yes, by all means breed Lady again. I can't see why the Davis farm doesn't bring an Arabian stud up from Kellogg's so that Northern California could benefit from it. I think it was a good idea to sell the old cart and get a new one. You can forget about putting the $100 away. I guess I used that up with unpaid gas at college. I hope those pictures are on their way by now.

Jack's War – Letters to home from an American WWII Navigator

School this week has been very hot and sultry. I am doing average work, nothing exceptional. I don't have to study as hard as most of the boys, and therefore I am enjoying my stay here much more. I am used to the army inefficiency now which also makes it easier. Dad, you would certainly be surprised at the way they handle the sick around here. The day I went out to one of the army flying fields where they measured me for shoes and where they take the sick, I rode right next to a boy with scarlet fever and another with measles right across from me. Please don't write back and ask me to be more careful because you don't ask why in the army, you just do it.

I went to a dance this Saturday with a Texas girl and had quite a time. These Texas girls are a lot different from California girls and I sure do like their drawl. Now remember please don't give me any lectures on morals in your next letters or my ensuing communique will be cut to a minimum with no military information at all. Well as they say in the army when they want you to keep still; "At ease Mister".

Jack

21 –June 20th, 1943 Sunday
Texas Tech College,
Lubbock, Texas
      Dear Mother and Dad,

Another week has slipped by without my knowing it. Time is really beginning to fly now. I guess it is because I am enjoying it every day.

About that money. Next time I will send by money order but for twelve years I have never had a letter lost or misplaced.

We have really been busy this week. Most of our free time has been taken up formations. Tuesday night we had to sign the payroll, Wednesday night we had the articles of war explained, Friday night we drilled for a parade which we had on Saturday and Thursday night we had a British military picture on keeping your mouth shut. This was the probably the most practical thing they've show us yet. Classes have been just the same.

In our Friday run we ran with another squadron which made about 240 men. I wasn't as successful as the last few times but did manage to take a third. The fellow who won is the rocky Mountain Conference champion in the two mile and he can really run.

You wanted to know about our classes. They are run exactly like college classes except we all march and stand at attention until given seats. Then we are just as natural as every day students.

Mother, please don't write and tell me what you expect of me when the war is over. I don't like lectures. All I want is news about what you are doing, and what our friend are doing. It doesn't bother me, but some boys have asked to be eliminated because their mother worried about them when they are flying.

I received the picture of Toots and it now sits on the dresser surrounded by pictures of my roommate's girlfriends. I wish those pictures of Koli would hurry up. I finally got some pictures taken, and I will send them to you as soon as they are developed.

Al Carter (Captain Carter's son) and I went dancing again this Saturday night. The girls we took ask for dinner this Sunday (tonight) and we really had a good time.

John Sproul and I have been writing to each other and he ended up in Albuquerque, New Mexico training to be a meteorologist.

Well there goes the whistle, so I'll turn in.

Jack's War – Letters to home from an American WWII Navigator

Jack

P.S. I hope you bred lady to Final Appeal. How are they getting along down on the farm with the Signal Corps there? I hope Stan Walley is better now. If you see them you can say hello for me.

22 – June 26th, 1943 Sunday
Texas Tech College,
Lubbock, Texas
Dear Mother and Dad,

Well first to acknowledge the pictures and nut which made a dull week seem bright. The pictures were exceptionally good and seemed as though I was right at home looking at Toots and you. The one of Mother, Jane and I reminded me of the nights we had company and Dad would insist on showing the pictures. The nuts were delicious and my roommates wish to thank you too. Please don't put off the "cookie idea" we don't care if they are spoiled. We would still eat them.

Dad, in your letter you mentioned that seven weeks had passed and some new development will take place soon. As far as I know, we stay here for five months or possibly four. You see I got in the thing just as the ball got rolling so we will be the first regular class and will stay the full five months.

Your weekend sounded like a good time to me. I enjoyed the note on mother's wanting to only buy "one" plant. I sure wish I could get home and see and ride Koli.

Our squadron "E" is what we call "on the beam". We won a parade march off yesterday and also room inspection. We are beating some of the boys who have been here longer than we have, and it kind of gets their goats.

We have had a test every day this week and it has been tough trying to find time to study.

These pictures are ones I have taken. The boy on my right is Captain Carter's son and the other is Harry Tritchmann, a boy from Idaho. The building is the one I live in. The building faces south.

Harry Tritchmann, Jack and Al Carter

Well we are going out again with our Texas gals so I'll have to leave.

Jack

Jack's War – Letters to home from an American WWII Navigator

23 – Monday June 28th, 1943
Texas Tech College,
Lubbock, Texas
Dear Mother and Dad,

Well I really had a close one this week. When we came back to the barracks Sunday night we were kept up to 11 o'clock signing a supplementary payroll. The next day we had to turn in all of our books. They had received a telegram from the Santa Ana or San Antonio that they were ready for 250 more boys.

Well there are a couple of squadrons ahead of us which are flying so they let them continue and took the next two squadrons and one to pre-flight that was academically good. Well that happened to be our flight so we were all elated with our meteoric rise. You see we would have gone to classification without ever taking flying. This would have meant that I would have been right there with Bob Griffith. Well here comes the sad part. They had seven men too many. So they took the last flight which was ours and took out the last seven men (alphabetically) and that meant me. All my friends I made at Sheppard (Al Carter) are leaving probably tomorrow. Oh well, that's the army. You're probably wondering why they would set up a system like this and then send 250 men who have just started it off to Classification.

Well this gives you a little idea of the importance of it. There are six of us left. I don't know what will happen to us, but we will fly a month earlier now. Let you know more later.

Jack

24 – Sunday July 4th, 1943
Texas Tech College,
Lubbock, Texas
Dear Mother and Dad,

Well a lot has really happened since I last wrote to you. I was certainly surprised when you wrote that I had been here for two months and something ought to be happening. I wrote back and said we would be here for our full five months and the next day they sipped almost every friend I have made in the army off to Santa Ana and left me here. Well what do you think happened to me?

They took the last man in flight 39 (alphabetically) and put him on flying schedule. That person was none other than I, and so without further ado I present you pilot John H. Woolsey who has been up more than three times to date. The first time was a thrill until I got sick. The second time I did not "urp" over the side, and the third time I never felt sick. As a flyer though, something tells me I better stick to horses. What I mean is that I can't get the hang of it and the instructor thinks I am pretty dumb. I hope I get over this for it certainly would be awful to wash out just because I couldn't fly.

The Democrat is now coming regularly and I enjoy reading it very much. Saw your name in the paper for installing Ernie Zebal in as President of Rotary.

I will ring if you insist, but I think letters and pictures are just as good and you can never think of what you want to say. Besides I will probably be at Santa Ana in three weeks. When I went on flying schedule they moved me up with another squadron but that's the army. I'm pretty sure of going to Santa Ana because they made this school a 9th Corps area two days ago and it used to be under the Gulf Coast command.

I guess you are in line for congratulations for ten of your most successful years. This is the half way mark for me too, ten years in San Francisco, and ten years in Woodland. By the way I really don't anything for my birthday *except* maybe a pen or some white wool socks or olive drab socks.

Jack

Jack's War – Letters to home from an American WWII Navigator

25 – Sunday, July 11th, 1943
Texas Tech College,
Lubbock, Texas

     Dear Mother and Dad,

     Things are coming along here plenty fast and again time is flying by. I received your book and am already half way through it. I wish I was half as interested in studies as I am in the "light reading". I am going to pass it on as you suggested. Also I received your card from Joe Di Maggio.

     I have been flying all this last week and I now have seven hours so you see I will be through flying this Thursday and either ship out this weekend or next (I hope). The flying gets more exciting and fun every time I'm up. I'm getting so I can really fly now and it sure is a good feeling. I will send you a little booklet on what I have learned and you will get an idea of what we are doing.

     We fly early in the mornings and in the afternoon. You really get a good idea of what Texas looks like. We have to keep our wits about us, for when the instructor says head back to the airport and you don't know where it is, it is very embarrassing. Yesterday was the most exciting day of all. I took the plane off and landed it nearly by myself. You see the instructor wants to live nearly as much as I do, so he always keeps his hands on the control. Yesterday we climbed up pretty high and did a few stalls. This is where you nose the plane up to where it can't climb anymore and start diving toward the ground. This is quite a thrill but the best of all is a "spin". You stall the plane exactly as before but just before it drops you kick the left rudder and the ship heads straight down spinning either right or left. You look straight down and count the spins as you come around. When you want to stop you give it the opposite rudder and the ship begins to dive. You then ease back on the stick and your plane goes like this.

40

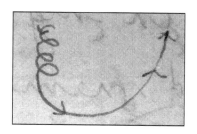

Drawing of recovery of a spiralling plane

When you start up, the gravity forces you down in your seat and the skin on your face seems as though it is crawling down your neck. At last you level off and everything returns to normal. The only trouble is that after diving a spinning normal flight seems like driving a car.

I guess I told you I dropped a few of my courses and am now taking Civil Air Regulations and First Aid. Surprisingly enough I know that first aid pretty well. I told you they had put me in another advanced academic section. When I went in they were just finishing up spherical trigonometry and were having a final test in two days. They made me take the final so I really had to cram being that I never had any in high school or college. Well I memorized a few formulas and said a prayer and pulled out a hundred percent much to the teacher's and my own amazement. This physics is going to be another story though I'm afraid.

Here are some pictures that I might not have sent. Looking forward to seeing those pictures of Kolie.

~~John~~ (that was a mistake everybody calls me John and they almost have me believing that's my name)

Jack

P.S. The other boy is Lynn Wilson my Texas roommate who is really one swell fellow.

Linn Wilson

Jack in front of his Barracks

Texas Tech "Barracks" 1943

Jack's War – Letters to home from an American WWII Navigator

26 – Sunday July 15, 1943
Texas Tech College,
Lubbock, Texas
> Dear Mother and Dad,

I have received everything sent and everything Is swell. The ring fits and looks plenty good and the cookies are practically all eaten up.

Even though I did not get to meet the "Wright Brothers", I had quite a birthday.

I want to warn you about my address. The whole thing must be written out in full with nothing omitted or left out especially "Squadron E, Section 39".

The reason for this was I was given a lecture this morning by the mail Sgt. Because Dad addressed the letter wrong. I was threatened with "tours" and told not to let it happen again.

Today is a banner day for today I finished my ten hours of flying. I really regret it, because I was really coming along fast. I had my last check flight on my birthday and scored an 89%. The highest mark they give is a 91% so I was quite thrilled. My instructor told me that another fellow and myself were the only ones out of ten he thought that had the makings of a pilot. He really gave me a good recommendation which I hope will help me in classification. He said I was calm, not nervous and really easy on the "stick". He said I was an earnest student and tried very hard. This was because I was worried so at first because I couldn't get on to it.

I would write up questions after each trip up and ask him the next day. I guess he liked this and he also liked the way I handled what they call forced landings. This is where they close the throttle and you have to pick out a field and glide in for a landing.

I am now ready to go to Classification and I hope I will leave in the next week or so. The main thing is to pass the "64" physical which is really tough on eyes. They ask you would you rather be a pilot, navigator or bombardier. I can't decide whether to put Navigator first and then Pilot or put Pilot first and then Navigator. Do you know anything about either one? Which would you put first? Well I have to make a formation so I'll close. I know this writing is terrible but I have been sitting on my bed. Would you please write a little plainer because I can't make out some of your words (enclosed small snippets of his father's writing).

Jack

27 – Sunday July 21st, 1943
Texas Tech College,
Lubbock, Texas
Dear Mother and Dad,

Boy! Oh! Boy! I received the pictures and the foal sure was a knockout. It has exceeded all expectations and I think it is the best picture we have of any of our horses. His head and ears are just perfect and he really looks like an Arabian. The light main shows up well too. It just seems as though I can reach out to touch him. I can just see him running over those hills out there with those other two horses trailing him. I can't wait to get home and ride him; he ought to be just about ready when I get my first furlough about 12 months from now if I don't get washed out at Santa Ana.

I have finished up practically all my courses and should ship by this weekend but there is a chance that I might be an "alternate" because I am out of another squadron. This means I would have to about a month and do nothing. I hope this won't happen though.

I'm just wondering what I should do if I get washed out at Santa Ana because of my eyes. They say there are some good things to get into but you have to act quick and pull all the strings you can. If I knew some officers at Santa Ana I could see, just in case I think it would help. Don't you know someone or somebody I could see there? I am really worried because I don't want to spend the rest of my career in the army as a private and that can easily happen.

We have just finished physics and boy what a test they did give us. You see I didn't have time to take electricity, magnetism and light so I didn't know anything.

Please thank the Eddy's for their delicious box of cookies. We certainly did enjoy them I will write them a letter later on.

I received a couple of nice handkerchiefs from Miss Ashburner and I am enclosing the $2 Grandpa sent me. Please tip him off that I can't and don't have time to cash checks in the army, especially in Texas.

I received $5 from Jane and also a very nice letter. She says something about you being interested in an Arabian stud from Kelloggs. This certainly sounds good to me. How much do they cost $500 or a $1000? Don't let Jane's talk about the quarter horse make you stray too far from the path of the Arabians. Just get a picture of Koli out or better yet go out and book him yourself.

Well I have to make retreat so I will say goodbye. I wouldn't write until you hear form me again.

Jack

P.S. Be sure and put my full address on always.

Note from Jack's father:

Jack phoned this afternoon. His voice normal but discouraged because his progress is so slow. His new flight flew onto Santa Ana- says he is just sitting around in his room. It cheered us up to hear his voice...

28 –August 1st, 1943
Texas Tech College,
Lubbock, Texas
        Dear Mother and Dad,

        Nothing new to report from Texas. I am still there just sitting around. I still take Physical Training and drill but that is all. I have been put on a few details due to the fact a few new men have arrived here, but besides that I just sit in my room reading. I have read <u>Withering Heights</u>, <u>The New York Yankees</u>, <u>Goodbye Mr Chips</u>, <u>20 Famous Short stories</u>, and about 32 of Guy de Maupassant's short stories. I am now starting <u>The Just and the Unjust</u> by James Gould Cozzens.

        While reading one day a Lt. came in and I asked what my chances were for getting a furlough. When I told him I had finished everything he said he didn't see anything else they could do with me. He told me to report the "Wing Headquarters" and see them about it. I had visions of living in California in few days so I got myself clean khakis and reported to WH. A sergeant asked me what I wanted and I told him. He then stuck his head in the Wing Commander's office. And said, "There's a kid out here who wants a furlough, he says he finished everything." The Lt., reading a book, just shakes his head and says "No soap". And so just like that they decided my fate.

        It kind of makes me sore the kind of baloney they feed these young fellows about the Air Corps. They ought to tell them the actual facts about their training and let it go at that.

        Well there really isn't much news so I'll close. Don't get the idea I'm down in the mouth about not being shipped, or that I'm not enjoying because that isn't the way I feel about it at all. It is just

Jack's War – Letters to home from an American WWII Navigator

that I have a lot of time on my hands which could be better spent than here at Texas Tech.

Jack

29 – August 7th, 1943
Texas Tech College,
Lubbock, Texas

Dear Mother and Dad,

Well here it is Sunday and it is just that much closer to the time we will ship. There have been some radical changes here lately. We have a new Company Commander Major Monroe from Colorado. Since we have come under the West Coast Command we have had a lot of inspections out this way, and they didn't think we were on the ball militarily so we are now getting it pushed down our throats. That is we are a great deal more regimented now than we were. The new Major told us he was trying to make this like West point.

Now I'm going to tell you something about what I have been doing since I have been here. Now I really mean this when I say don't let this go any further than you. I have been a student officer in our squadron (120 men). I am what they call an adjutant or second in command. It gives one a lot of practice in how to handle men and I wouldn't trade it for anything. Some of the things we do, I wouldn't necessarily agree with, but you can't change the army. We have to wear little red badges and the boys have to salute up and we also eat at a separate table during mess. Of course there are the disadvantages too. The real officers of the detachment are expecting us to be examples so we have to be especially careful and dress just right or we get sacked for it. It is amazing to me how I was chosen for I am about as unmilitary as they come and don't agree with their ideas half the time. Well just remember what I said about this being kept quiet and please don't give me any excuses about "you thought it would be all right to tell so and so because". I don't want it to go any further than you two.

We had a very sad accident out at the airport this week. One of the fellows in my squadron was out flying and his [plane went into a tight spin and they couldn't pull out. The boy was from Idaho and one of the best liked fellows in the squadron. We all got together and collected $150, and we are sending a big floral piece, and also going to buy a foot stone with an inscription on it.

We might ship this coming weekend but I doubt it, probably the next weekend. I received your letter and approve of the letter you sent to Col. Lee and thank you very much for doing it. I receive the Democrat quite regularly now.

That powered lawnmower sound like the ticket to me even if it is about five years too late. Your trip to Monticello makes my mouth water. I haven't seen a decent sized mountain in about four months and I am getting sick and tired of Texas. Well it won't be long now. I hope...

Jack

P.S. Note new address

A/S (Aviation student) We are just plain privates but the army likes to kid us.

30 – August 16th, 1943
Texas Tech College,
Lubbock, Texas
Dear Mother and Dad,

Well here is the day we are supposed to ship on and we're not shipping. I am getting used to it. The trouble seems to be they can't get a train for us. But we will probably go in the next two days.

Jack's War – Letters to home from an American WWII Navigator

It sure makes me mad that Hollis went a month later than I did and is now at Santa Ana.

I have received everything you sent me; cookies, peanuts and book. Thank you very much. I am saving the book to read on the train if we ever ship. I am certainly glad to hear Toots is better. I think she needs about two weeks in the mountains, and oh boy, I wish I could spend just one day at Feather River Meadows. We have just been drilling in the hot sun for almost a week and I do mean hot. The perspiration just runs off.

This morning the students put all the student officers in a mud hole out on the athletic field. I fought as hard as I could but there were too many and they soon overpowered me and threw me into it. Luckily I had on my gym equipment.

Well, I'll drop you a line when I get to Santa Ana.

About coming down there to see me; I am confined to the barracks for fourteen days and to the Post for forty two days. I can have visitors after the fourteen days but can't go off the post. I really think a trip like that is rather unnecessary, and I would prefer you wait until I get a furlough or I am at one of the schools that actually fly.

Jack

31 – August 22nd, 1943
Texas Tech College,
Lubbock, Texas
     Dear Mother and Dad,

Well another Sunday is come and I am still here at dear old Texas Tech. I will no doubt be here for the duration or six months. We were supposed to ship last Monday, but the due to big

50

westward troop movements there were no cars available for us. We are supposed to ship tomorrow for sure but I doubt it very much.

When we do go we are going on Pullmans under the leadership of student officers. My roommate Linn Wilson who is the head student officer of the whole detachment is going to be train commander and under him will be seven car commanders of which I am one. I am responsible for the welfare and conduct of the men in my car. I have to confiscate any liquor brought on board, and make sure none of them run off the train at any of the stops and also they don't whistle or shout at girls (that is going to be hard to stop).

I finished <u>Will Rogers</u> and really enjoyed it, for all that I knew of him before was that he played in the movies and wrote "Will Rogers Says".

I sure appreciate you registering Koli for me. I don't know why but I never seemed to get around to it.

I can't wait to see the pictures of Koli and certainly do hope that you don't stop taking pictures until it is impossible to get film.

I know I always "kick" when you bring them out, but that is for the company's sake. I just can't see why they would be interested in our horses, but that is just me. I hope you are taking good care of Toots and if they operate I hope you are there if something should go wrong. Mother, I think even you should go with her in case they do operate so she won't get panicky.

Well, I hope the next time I write it will be from Santa Ana for I am getting tired of hearing how Texas is winning the war by itself. They also are still fighting the civil war down here and "damyankee" is one word.

Jack

Jack's War – Letters to home from an American WWII Navigator

Chapter 4

Classification Center

Santa Ana

32 – August 26th, 1943
Santa Ana Army Air Base
Santa Ana, California
(This appears to be a pre written form for families)

Dear Mother and Dad,

I am sending this from Classification Center here at the Santa Ana Army Air Base, where I arrived today. I was met at the train and am now with the rest of the future Army Air crews.

I've been registered and assigned to Squadron 12, where I shall remain for about two weeks. During that time I will have my physical examinations and tests which will determine whether I become a Pilot, Bombardier, or Navigator. After being classified, my actual pre-flight training begins. That pre-flight training will last for about nine weeks and then I will be sent to one of the flying schools to start my training.

You will, no doubt, think it strange receiving this type of letter from me instead of a personal note, but here is the reason why: Our Commanding Officer knows that during the excitement and process of getting settled during the next few days, some of us will be apt to forget to write the folks at home. This is his way of letting you know where I am and that I am well. It is just one of the many indications that I will be taken care of in the Army Air Forces. Another is my protection by National Service Life Insurance which is granted me free of charge all through my training period.

I know I'll have more nice things to tell you when I write a real letter. In the meantime, please let me hear from you. My Address is

Jack's War – Letters to home from an American WWII Navigator

Squadron 12
Army Air Base
Santa Ana, California
P.S. Just arrived this morning. I am now being processed.

August 31st 1943

From Jack's Father

Jack phoned from Santa Ana

This call came about 11 A.M. I could hear his voice very clearly. And he seemed happy to be back in California and as excited as I was.

33 – August 25th, 1943
Santa Ana Army Air Base
Santa Ana, California
Dear Mother and Dad,

Well this is going to be hard to believe, but we are actually on our way to Santa Ana. Right now we are approaching Gallop New Mexico where we will eat our breakfast.

We turned in all our bedding Tuesday morning and signed all necessary slips and were packed ready to go by 2:00. We ate supper at 5:30 and then marched to the train which was a quarter of a mile away. The train consisted of seven cars and of course an engine. There are two hundred fifty of us on board with thirty six to a car. Student officers are in complete charge of a car as planned. I am the car commander of Car #1, which is right behind the engine. I am rather lucky for being car commander and I have the compartment with my assistant which is rather classy to say the least.

We had an uneventful night although I didn't sleep too well. We all arose at 6:00 A.M. rather the conductor woke me and I awoke the car. I then dressed and shaved in my private bathroom like any millionaire would do.

The little I could see of Texas last night before it became too dark was flat and covered with sage brush. What a pleasant surprise to wake up in the morning and take in the mountains of New Mexico. They aren't like our coast range or the Sierras, but they are really pretty. They are cut off at the top forming mesas and they also have red cliffs. They aren't covered with tall trees but with sage brush and greasewood. Practically all of the houses are made of adobe and you would be surprised at the number of hovels you see. I saw some real Navajo Indians earlier this morning and they were all dressed up in bright colored clothes as if there might be some celebrations going on.

We will be pulling into gallop soon so I will close and write again.

Jack

34 – September 5th, 1943
Santa Ana Army Air Base
Santa Ana, California
Dear Mother and Dad,

This is the first chance I have had since arriving to write a letter. They have really kept us busy trying to classify us. It has been very interesting to me and perhaps you would like to hear about it too, but I wouldn't say too much about it, for it is supposed to be a military secret for some reason or other.

The first day we arrived we were hauled to Santa Ana from the station in a fleet of trucks. We filled out blanks by the hundreds all afternoon. That night we "G.I'd" the barracks. I can't remember

Jack's War – Letters to home from an American WWII Navigator

what we did Friday but it wasn't very important. On Saturday we had a personal inspection which was very rigid especially on shoes. On next Monday we started what they call our M days. I don't know what the M means but we have 15 of these days until we are classified. Each day we have certain duties and tests to take on each of them, with the first week being the most important.

Back to Monday. This day we had four lectures. In the morning we were welcomed to Santa Ana and explained all about the processes and in the afternoon we were given a close up on the duties of each member of the air crew (P. B. or N.). Tuesday was one of our toughest. We had eight hours of aptitude tests. These tests were not to find out our depth of knowledge, but to find out our ability to perform simple processes and the speed with which we can do it. After coming out of that building that night, I think I can understand why doctors get tired just working in hospitals. Wednesday we had the Psycho-motor test which tested our coordination and the speed of our reactions. I can't tell you about all of the test, but it was more or less like a penny arcade. One of them was turning pegs half way around in a certain time. They were square pegs set in square holes. We had to lift them out, turn them half way around and set them back in again. This was the simplest of any. Also that day we had an urinalysis, blood test, and a shot to see whether we were susceptible to "desert fever". Also we had a dentist check, and I am going to have a wisdom tooth pulled.

Thursday we filled out blanks stating illnesses and diseases and operations we had and then we had an interview with a psychologist which was very important and they really dug down into your personal life. One boy admitted he had a few headaches at Texas Tech and they washed him right out. They gave me a number somewhere in the hundreds, mine was 666. All those who had an odd middle number were immediately washed out. The next day we took our "64" Physical and needless to say I didn't get much sleep the night before. We were to take it Friday afternoon, being at the end of the alphabet. All during that morning I was just praying my eyes would be right. When you report to the flight surgeon to receive your papers to go through to the "64" there is a white slip of paper at the top right corner if you have washed out on the aptitude or the psychomotor and I was just a little scared for that morning several good friends of mine had received the white slip and had washed out of air crew.

Well, I didn't get the white slip so preceded onto the "64". We first were checked for night vision which I just passed by the skin of my teeth. We then had the "Schnider" which I passed without taking the phenobarbitol. We then were checked to see if we were all there. I mean I had to stand on one foot and all that stuff. We then went to the eye department and I passed with 20/20 in each eye. I guess I got through the whole test for I didn't have to take any rechecks at all. You might be interested to know that one fellow had 160 B.P. so I let him have one of my Phenobarbital tablets and he passed with 132. We lost about 40 out of 250 men on the aptitude and psycho-motor and only one or two on the physical. We aren't all through yet but, I think we are all through with the tests and I think I will be classified. We now get details and lectures until next Saturday when we will find out what we are classified as. I will either telephone you Saturday afternoon, night or Sunday. Thanks for the book and the magazine. I think I will enjoy the book immensely. Well I have to get ready for the parade this afternoon. I am enclosing a letter they gave us a sample of how we eat here. The letter isn't bad but just a bit misleading. I certainly could use a pen if there is a spare one around the house. Well I'll see you later.

Jack

P.S. sending letters and stuff under separate envelope

Note Jack's comment about the author being an idealist

Note from Jack's Father:

Jack phoned at 6:50 AM. He reports he has been classified as a bombardier. He was happy to have made the "air crew" but was, we take it, primarily interested in navigation. He is well- and above all happy to be back in California with old friends.

35 – September 15th, 1943
Santa Ana Army Air Base
Santa Ana, California
Dear Mother and Dad,

Well were still in the classification area but things are beginning to happen. As you know I was classified Bombardier as was my friend Linn. We found out it wasn't a bad deal at all and that you received some navigation, but we still had our hearts set on being navigators. Yesterday we went down to the classification centre and walked up to the Captain's secretary and said we had been told by the Captain to come and see him. We were ushered in in front of several others as though he has been expecting us. We saluted and immediately went to work on him and did not leave until we were reclassified navigators. So! We are now navigators. I guess we will still go to pre-flight here, but one can ever tell. We will receive five weeks of "aerial gunnery" for all Navigators and Bombardiers are gunners now.

I was on a small detail the other day which began at 3:45am and lasted till 8:15pm. They call it Mess Management there, we call it K.P.

I did pretty well for I was "Bowl and Sink" man and handled 3000 bowls without an error. I think the New York Yankees would be interested in me.

I just received a marvellous travelling bag from Uncle Leon, it is the envy of the whole barracks. You can't even get one like it in the P.X.'s down here.

I sure wish I could get a couple of days off but they don't even know what the word "furlough" means. One fellow in the whole pre-flight area got a 3-day pass and that was because his wife wrote the Colonel and told him she could get only one furlough a

Jack's War – Letters to home from an American WWII Navigator

year for she was in the Air Transport Command. I see Hollis and Bob most every night and went to a show with Hollis last night. They are both in pre-flight and Bob is leaving for Primary soon. Well we're having P.T. in an hour so I'll close.

Jack

36 – September 21st, 1943
Santa Ana Army Air Base
Santa Ana, California

Dear Mother and Dad,

Here I am stalled again. We moved into a pool squadron for Bombardiers and Navigators and it will probably be two to three weeks before we move onto pre-flight. In the meantime we just drill and take physical training. There are about ten to twelve boys who don't give a dam about anything and therefore cause the whole squadron to devote their free time to drilling. I guess we will appreciate our commissions that much more if we can get them. We have a 50-50 chance of taking our pre-flight in Texas at Ellington field, but I hope we take it here.

Linn Wilson's aunt came out to visit him last Sunday and brought a picnic lunch with them. He invited me to go down to the reception center with him and eat lunch.

I received the candy and it really was good. Anything you can send will be appreciated by us all. I also received five dollars and again thank you. I think I shall invest it in a pen.

Say dad, if you can get a hold of some good double edged razor blades, please send them to me for we are in dire need of them. The blades they sell in the army can't cut soft butter and we get gigged every time we aren't shaved.

Tomorrow we are going through the "pressure chamber". This tests our reaction to high altitude. They take us up to 18,000' for ten minutes. If you pass out they wash you out. They take you up to 38,000' with oxygen masks on for an hour.

Don't forget to change my Democrat address.

Jack

37 – September 26th, 1943

Santa Ana Army Air Base
Santa Ana, California

Dear Mother and Dad,

By the time this letter reaches you I will be well on my way to Texas, but not Lubbock. This time it is to Ellington Field, Houston Texas where we will take our pre-flight. I don't think it will be bad at all for they say the food is good and so is the climate.

We went through the pressure chamber the other day and I didn't have any trouble at all. First they took us up to 5000' to clear our ears, then to 18000' without oxygen for fifteen minutes. We then went to38, 000' for fifteen minutes and then we came down to 30,000' for an hour. We were then finished. Lots of the boys had trouble and got the bends. It certainly gave you an idea of the necessity of oxygen over 10,000'.

We have been doing nothing except drill and P.T. lately. We will become aviation cadets Monday when we ship. You can see by the money order that I was paid yesterday.

I just finished 30 seconds over Tokyo and I really enjoyed it. I sure do appreciate a book every once in a while, and also the candy.

I am now reading Elmer Gantry a book by Sinclair Lewis which promises to be very amusing. I don't expect to have much time in pre-flight though.

See you in Texas,
Jack

38 – October 3rd, 1943
Santa Ana Army Air Base
Santa Ana, California

Dear Mother and Dad,

Please excuse the delay in writing but I have been so mad and done so little that I just couldn't write.

We have been doing those silly little details that the army thinks up for you when you are a holdover. They moved in about a hundred navigators last Friday so we are starting to drill and take P.T. again. It feels just like going back to high school, for we have already done this.

Jack's War – Letters to home from an American WWII Navigator

I received the razor blades and they are plenty good. I also enjoyed the Reader's Digest. I am now just finishing <u>Guadalcanal Diary</u> I also just finished <u>Elmer Gantry</u> by Sinclair Lewis which was very funny.

I hope you are still coming down this weekend for I will get my first pass. You can meet me at the reception center. I think I will be free to leave between 1:00 and 2:00 and will have till about 2:30 Sunday. I just booked my dentist appointment and it will come Friday and they are going to pull a wisdom tooth but I think I will be alright.

Nothing new so I will close.

Jack

Oct 11th, 1943

The report from Jack's father on the visit at Santa Ana:

Just returned from a wonderful visit with Jack. He is a bit thinner and sort of leathery looking from the Texas sun. He has a wonderful sense of humor and is more tolerant of other's ideas and shows determination to accomplish that for which he originally set out. His special request "let me see and be near some trees and see the ocean" more always. He was pleased to get behind the wheel of the car. We had dinner at Knott's Berry Farm, drove home by the ocean; had a room together at the Santa Ana Hotel; showed the "kodachromes", and some movies: a delicious repast of berry jam cake , cookies and iced berry juice prepared by Beth; to bed at 10:30 and up at 8:30; breakfast at the grill; a drive around Santa Ana's nicest homes; some picture taking; and eventually reached the air base gate at 2:20; and again with controlled emotions said goodbye. The trip was most worthwhile.

Dad

Oct 9th 1943 Jack in Santa Ana

Jack and his mother Beth Woolsey

Jack's War – Letters to home from an American WWII Navigator

39 – October 16th, 1943
Santa Ana Army Air Base
Santa Ana, California

Dear Mother and Dad,

It's Sat. afternoon again but it seems like Years instead of a week since you were outside the gate.

This week has been extremely interesting for in this stage of navigator training we made an extensive study of "K.P.". It seems as though we were lucky and got K.P. four times this week. I think this is some sort of record. After the second day (15hrs/day) I noticed that there were at least twenty boys who never appeared on the list, so I got to thinking that I ought to be one of those twenty for I am not one to hog all the K.P. Well, I spotted our corporal and casually asked him if there wasn't some small detail he could put me on, but there wasn't much chance unless I was a carpenter for the Captain wanted a Bookcase built!

This was my only chance so I quickly assured him that I had four years' experience and that my father was a carpenter before me. I was taken off the K.P. list immediately and needless to say it took me three days to build this masterpiece. After the first coat of paint it looked pretty good, but I managed to find one spot which wasn't and took the rest of the day to give the whole bookcase a second coat. Besides getting out of K.P. the Captain thinks I am a good guy now and is going to make sure I am on the next shipping list.

Hollis and I are going to meet Bob in L.A. tonight and then we are going to celebrate for the last time tonight for this is the last time we will be together. Well it's getting time to go by and get Hollis so I'll close. Say hello to Toots and give her my usual two chops.

Jack

HEADQUARTERS
SANTA ANA ARMY AIR BASE
OFFICE OF THE COMMANDING OFFICER
SANTA ANA, CALIFORNIA

18 Oct 43

Dear Dr. Woolsey,

I have been informed that your son, John Homer Woolsey, has been selected by the Classification Board for training as a Navigator in the Army Air Forces. I congratulate both you and him on this achievement.

The position of the Navigator is one of utmost importance in the combat team. The Pilot and Bombardier are dependent upon his skill and speed in making necessary calculations to insure the success of the mission, and the safety of the entire crew is dependent upon his accuracy and reliability under all conditions.

He will soon be assigned to one of the Army Air Forces West Coast Training Center navigation schools for an intensive course of instruction. We confidently expect him to successfully complete this course and to receive his Wings and rating as a qualified Navigator.

It is my hope that you will derive great satisfaction from the selection of your son for this important training and that his future career in the Army Air Forces will be one of continuing success and service.

Sincerely yours,

W. A. ROBERTSON,
Colonel, Army Air Forces,
Commanding

Jack's Official Acceptance into the Navigation Program

Oct 18th, 1943

From Jack's Father:
Jack just phoned. I was at the house alone. He is very excited. He leaves for Ellington Field near Houston today at noon. When he leaves he automatically becomes an aviation cadet.
Dad

Chapter 5

Ellington Field Texas

Navigation School

40 – October 21st, 1943
Group 25, AFPS
Navigator Wing
Ellington Field Texas
          Dear Mother and Dad,

We arrived at Ellington today after a wonderful trip down here. We were not allowed to write on the way so consequently this is the first chance I've had since Monday afternoon.

We went on a more southern route than the one I came out on. We went through Los Angeles and had a seven hour layover. We woke Tuesday just as we passed over the Colorado River into Arizona. We went thru Phoenix, Tucson and passed very close to the Mexican border, and went thru Hachita and Columbus in New Mexico and then El Paso, Monahan, Big Springs, Sweetwater, Abilene, Fort Worth and Dallas and Houston. When some Texans ever question the legality of calling a thousand acre piece of land a "ranch" in California, I just remind them that it takes one hundred thousand acres in Texas to equal that one thousand acres in productivity.

The country around Houston is very much like Woodland. A little north of Houston there is quite a lot of pine which is something in Texas. I think the strangest thing I saw was the "negro mammies" picking cotton with a bag over their shoulder. The cattle in western Texas weren't very fat and did not look as of good grade as the northern type.

Ellington is something of a paradise compared to Santa Ana. They treat us like men instead of Boy Scouts, and there is absolutely no K.P. for cadets.

We really can't say what our schedule will be but I will write when I find out.

Linn Wilson came over this evening and greeted me in true Texan style with a "Howdy Pahdner". It sure was good seeing him again. He assures me Ellington is an all right place. Well I have to go to bed and catch up on some of that sleep I lost on the train.

Jack

41 – October 24th, 1943
Group 25, AFPS
Navigator Wing
Ellington Field Texas
Dear Mother and Dad,

Just a note to let you know I am still in Texas. We have spent a very uneventful four days doing practically nothing which is remarkable. The food is a dam sight better than Santa Ana, but we are still on Field Rations which means that we will receive $84 instead of the regular $75, but I can use it for I am going to buy a few clothes, and we have to look and dress better for we are cadets now and that is a rank between a warrant officer and a sergeant.

So far we have been treated swell, but we are holding our breaths. This pre-flight is run on the class system. The first three weeks we are underclass men, and the cadets on their last three weeks are our officers. The second three weeks are on our own and have our own officers, and the last three weeks we are the officers to the incoming cadets.

This coming week the Rice College girls are giving us a tea dance on Sunday at one of Houston's big hotels. Oh Boy! I'm sure

Jack's War – Letters to home from an American WWII Navigator

going to be there. We are supposed to get two weekend overnight passes. That is from Saturday 3:00 P.M. to Sunday 10:00 P.M. I would like to spend one with the Leakes if possible. How should I go about it?

Most of the boys are living in regular two story barracks, but all the (W's) are living in single story tar paper shacks which aren't bad at all. They are long and have eight men to each room.

I can't get a pen so if you do, please send it down. Also I could use that electric razor being as we don't have much time to shave and the latrine is always crowded in the morning. Well I have to get to bed so I'll be ready for classes in the morning.

Jack

42 – October 30th 1943
Group 25, AFPS
Navigator Wing
Ellington Field Texas
    Dear Mother and Dad,

Well we have just completed our first week and they really kept us busy. Here's a rough schedule of our day. Reveille at 5:10 breakfast at 6:00 "March On" at 7:30 (this is a short parade just before we go to classes.) 8:00 to 9:00 Aircraft Identification, 9:00 to 10:00 Code, 10:00 to 11:00 Physics, 11:00 to 12:00 Math, lunch at 12:15. 1:40 to 2:45 Physical Training, 3:00 to 4:00 Drill, 4:00 to 5:00 Drill and retreat; 6:00 Dinner, 7:00 to 10:00 study or free time.

Being that this was our first week they took all our free time for necessary formations. I think it will get easier as we go on. Aircraft Identification is harder than I thought. We study the plane such as the armament, wing span (this is for the later use when sighting with machine guns) horse power, speed, rate of climb etc.

Then they flash a picture on a screen for a $1/10^{th}$ of a second and we are supposed to recognize it. We practice by flashing five and 6 digit numbers on the screen for 1/100 of a second and then write them down. Code is plenty hard too. We sit there with earphones on and "dit dah's" singing in our ears and are supposed to remember what they mean. We have to pass ten words a minute by the end of the course. Physics and math are going to be the easiest, for I have had these before. P.T. is really rough all we do is exercise and wind sprints and after we get them with them we have to drill for two hours. It isn't so hard to swallow though because everyone is civil and they aren't always shouting at us.

The Code and Aircraft Identification are the hardest, and they are really clamping down now and washing them out if they don't pass with average over 70%.

Well I'm going into town tonight to have a look-see.

Sunday morning

Boy! Am I tired. Late nights are one of things the army does not prepare you for. Houston seems like a very good town but didn't get much of a chance to look it over. We got into town about 4:00 and looked over the downtown district. Then we ate dinner and went to "For Whom the Bells Toll" which was extra good. We then went up to the cadet and offices club where we had something to drink. We had to be back on the field by 12:00 so we caught the bus and came home. This afternoon the girls are giving us a tea dance so we can get acquainted. Well that's about all the news. Of course I'm interested in cookies or nuts. Remember I told you I wanted them anytime.

Jack

P.S. I ran into two old classmates of mine who are Bombardiers going through pre-flight here. One is Harold Adams and the other is Ernie Bottarie who played Right Half for us in 1940.

Jack's War – Letters to home from an American WWII Navigator

I think he changed his name to Pierucci that year. You can find them in my "Ilex" if you are interested.

43 – November 6th 1943
Group 25, AFPS
Navigator Wing
Ellington Field Texas
    Dear Mother and Dad,

    This is Saturday afternoon and we have just finished a big parade honouring four wives whose husbands are missing in action.

    We had a stiff inspection but our room pulled through due to a G.I. party (scrubbing and cleaning) we had last night. Before I forget I have received the book, papers, Readers Digest, electric razor and pen which are quite satisfactory. The razor is coming in handy for I don't have to stand in line in the mornings. The book is amazing but to tell you the truth, I don't have time to read. I sure could use those shorts and socks you told me about.

    We haven't been wearing any different uniform unless it is cold. We had a cold spell, and we put on our olive drab just like the G.I. Army. The only thing different about our uniform is our service cap which they are going to issue us this week. They look something like this.

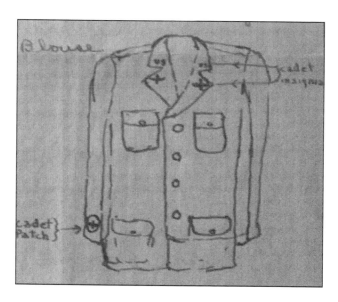

Jack's Uniform

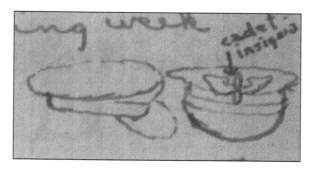

Jack's hat

When going to town we wear our O.D. pants, a khaki shirt and our blouse.

The courses are getting pretty stiff, but the only one that will give me much trouble is Code. We have had a Physics, Math and Aircraft Identification test and I have passed them all with good marks, but this Code is going to be a different story.

That is certainly too bad about Aunt Bessie. I hope she gets over it. I had a letter from Bob and he told me all about his solo flight. Sometimes I wish I had asked for pilot, but this is getting pretty interesting and I am learning something of value after seven months of just preparing.

I received a Democrat with my right address on it which is nothing short of a miracle, and I hope they keep surprising me. I know that girl that Jim Sutherland married, and she is pretty all right. I am kind of surprised at Nancy Merritt, but I think the war had a lot to do with it.

If you could let me have a pair of garters I would appreciate it for they are pretty hard to buy down here and they check on us to see if we are wearing them. I received a post card from Mrs Leake and a letter from Dr Leake this Sunday. A bus goes right by Ellington and it only takes an hour to get there.

Those four pursuit planes that flew over the parade in Woodland were P39s. Bell is the manufacturer, and Airacobra is their name. We are cutting down their numbers because they are outmoded. It was one of the first to have a cannon firing through the nose and the Russians praise it very highly.

Well it is getting around that time for us to fall out for our personal inspections before going into town. Needless to say that tea dance last Sunday was a roaring success with plenty of Texan belles. Well say hello to Toots if you get a chance.

Jack

Aviation cadet JHW
AF Air Forces Pre-flight School
Group 25 Navigator,
Squadron F Flight 4

44 – Post card undated

Dear Folks,

Just got back from a wonderful visit with the Leakes. Caught a bus and arrived there in just one hour and fifteen minutes. A tornado had just struck that night and kind of battered the town up. The Leake's windows (just two) and a door were smashed but otherwise no damage. Chauncey is at Roswell Military Academy but Wilson was home sick but recovering. Had a swell dinner and Dr Leake showed me the medical school which is very good. They gave me chicken and waffles and said to be sure to say hello. They have a beautiful house, but "Praise the Lord" we live in California. Well tempus fugit (space vanishes) so...

Jack

45 – Ellington Field Texas
November 15th, 1943
Group 25, AFPS
Navigator Wing
Dear Mother and Dad,

This letter is a little late but there is actually very little news from Texas. I spent the weekend studying up on my Physics so I could get a good grade in my second test. I cracked a hundred in my first and I figure if I can pile up some good grade in Maths & Physics it will balance out my marks in Code.

Right now it is raining and we have to sign the payroll, and you can imagine at what end of the line the "Ws" are. Just received the cookies & nuts, and to say that they were delicious is a triumph of understatement. The boys I live with get food from their parents and we usually manage to have a feed after the Friday nite G.I party. One fellow is from the Bronx and his folks sent him some

"Kosher salami" so you can see we have quite a variety. The boys were especially enthusiastic about the salted almonds.

I am sending a package home and in it is a flight jacket. We can't wear them until we are officers and are not allowed to have them in our possession. This one fellow had one and sold it to me cheap and it would really be a good jacket to have after the war. If you can wear it, Dad, go ahead. You better get it cleaned first.

Do you remember my friend Linn Wilson, well he is Wing Commander of the Navigator Wing which is the highest position in the Cadet Officer, here is a rough idea of the set up here at Ellington.

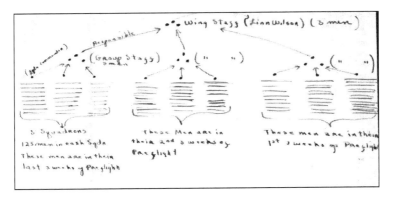

Pre-Flight Squadrons

I hope you can make this out so you will get the idea of how they run things down here. That's about all the news from the gulf so give my regards to Toots and keep the cookies coming.

Jack

46 – November 21st, 1943
Group 25, AFPS
Navigator Wing
Ellington Field Texas
Dear Mother and Dad,

Here it is Sunday night and I'm sitting on the edge of my bunk with my barracks bag stretched out by the heater. I guess you get the idea, Dad! I sure do envy you and wish I was there to enjoy our home and dog. I just saw "Lassie, Come Back" which has a beautiful collie in it and the beautiful scenes reminded me of the summer that Toots and I spend at Mt. Lassen.

This week has been very uneventful. We finished up our math Friday and start on "Maps and Charts" tomorrow. Code is becoming easier but I am by no means out of danger.

I received the socks and underwear and also the chocolates which were very good. I'm looking forward to that book for I have read several articles on Joe Foss. I have received two Democrats with the night address the rest have been forwarded from S.A. I would appreciate it if you would enlighten them to my whereabouts.

I just wrote Grandpa and Uncle Leon a letter, and feel a telegram is a little unnecessary as I have no sensational news that I haven't included in the letters. We have about two telephones to about one thousand men and you sign up weeks before to use it and this is the only way to get a telegram off.

Mother wondered if I'd be home for Christmas – I have explained about furloughs before, only cadets with a year service are even considered.

You keep asking for pictures and I feel this needs an explanation. We are not allowed cameras on the field. We get to town around 4:00 Saturday afternoon and we are usually the last four squadrons in. The studios are filled by then so we just don't

Jack's War – Letters to home from an American WWII Navigator

have a chance to get a picture. I'll keep trying though. I wish you would give me an idea of what you want for Christmas so I could have time to look around down here. Speaking of calling, Dickey Stephens; John, that's what they all call me too. Well that's all the news.

Jack

47 – November 28th, 1943
Group 25, AFPS
Navigator Wing
Ellington Field Texas
      Dear Mother and Dad,

      Just completed our fifth week of pre-flight and have only four more to go. We finished Physics this week and now take up Naval courtesies and customs along with ship identification. My courses now are Aircraft Identification, Code, Naval Identification and Maps and Charts which is a very practical course. We learn about the different projections and how to read navigational charts, which is going to help us at advance school. In the afternoon we have a course on small arms which take up the Thompson Sub Machine Gun andthe Calibre 45 Pistol which we will fire on the range pretty soon.

      I passed an eight word code test the other day and I am now on ten so I think I'll get by okay. I finished Math with a ninety five average, but it is pretty easy.

      Thanksgiving was an average day except for our night meal which was just like any Thanksgiving meal with Turkey and dressing and all the things that go with it.

      I can't think of anything I want for Christmas for I have just about everything I need. I would like to come home but I can't. You have to have a year's service before you can apply for one so that is that.

Well there just isn't any more news so I'll close,

Jack

48 – December 4th, 1943
Group 25, AFPS
Navigator Wing
Ellington Field Texas
Dear Mother and Dad,

Just finished Sat morning inspection and the parade was called off because of the weather, we have had quite a bit of rain lately.

This past week has been very good for me, for I had quite a surprise. I passed my ten word check in code and then passed "sending" which finishes my requirements for Code. We have to pass fourteen words before we are exempted, but we can take it all the way through advanced. I am now working on twelve words which just seems like a bunch of dit dahs coming at you as fast as they can. We took our final in Air Craft Identification yesterday and I managed to get forty six planes out of the fifty which gave me a ninety two which stands as our grade in A.I.

Linn Wilson and his group are moving out today to "Advance Navigation". Linn going across the field to Advanced which is a darn good deal. The rest are going to "Hondo" and "San Marcus" and some to gunnery. It looks as though they send all the student officers to Ellington and the rest to other schools and gunnery, so being that I'm not a student officer and I doubt if I'll go here.

We sure did appreciate that wonderful box Mother, all the boys sure like those nuts and the cake was delicious to. We had

Jack's War – Letters to home from an American WWII Navigator

some Kosher Chicken to go with it. Ha! Well this is about all the news for now.

Jack

49 – December 11th, 1943
Group 25, AFPS
Navigator Wing
Ellington Field Texas
      Dear Mother and Dad,

      Just another weekly letter to let you know that your California son loves Woodland and would give his right arm to be back there enjoying Christmas with you. The Leakes have asked me down for Christmas dinner and that will come on Saturday, the day after we graduate, and I hope I will be able to make it but there is a chance we might ship to advanced or gunnery.

      This week has been pretty interesting due to the fact we fired on the range with the 45 pistol. We practiced on the range with the 45 pistol. We practiced one day and shot for score the next. This goes on our service record so it means quite a bit. We fired ten rounds at fifteen yards rapid fire, ten rounds twenty five yards slow and rapid fire, fifteen rounds at a bobbing target. I think there were three of us out of our whole flight who qualified. There are three classes in which you qualify in, Expert, Sharpshooter and Marksman. I was marksman which isn't the best but helps on the record due to the fact that only 15% of all cadets qualify. We're supposed to get medals like that to wear; perhaps you've seen some on the soldiers.

Marksman medal

The Democrat is coming regularly and it was kind of nice to read. Maybe we can subscribe to it when I get to advanced. I received mother's nuts & cake which were delicious, but I have failed to receive "Joe Foss" or any pictures which were promised but I guess they're on the way.

That certainly was swell that Bob got home. It sure would be nice if I was stationed at Mather Field.

The army gave us four sulphanilamide pills to build up our resistance for colds. Then the next day we drilled in the rain.

Say hello to Toots and write more letters.

Jack

50 – December, 1943
Group 25, AFPS
Navigator Wing
Ellington Field Texas
    Dear Mother and Dad,

I just received your letter today and am worried about what to do about the wedding. I would like to send a telegram to Mr. and Mrs. Claude? (I don't even know his last name). From what I can gather they are getting married in our house on Saturday what time (I don't know). We are not allowed to send congratulatory message

Jack's War – Letters to home from an American WWII Navigator

in telegrams on night letters. I hope you will understand the situation down here. We are bottled up with restrictions and rules which make it hard to use a phone or send a telegram. You tell your tactical officer that your sister is getting married, and you would like permission to phone a telegram in and he says if we let every cadet do this we would etc! etc! etc! I will write a letter and enclose it in this one and you can give it to them for me.

I hope everything goes okay and you have a good time. I will be thinking about "you all". Rumor has it that we're getting a two and a half day pass at Christmas and I don't know what to do yet, but I think I will visit some town in Texas if I stay on the post.

Jack

(Also in the same envelope):

I've racked my brain for something to say, but I can't think of anything that doesn't sound silly – so you will have to do it for me

Jack

51 – December 19th, 1943
Group 25, AFPS
Navigator Wing
Ellington Field Texas
Dear Mother and Dad,

I have just returned from Houston after spending Saturday night and Sunday there. We had our graduation dance Saturday night at the Rice Hotel and most of us boys had rooms there for we were given an overnight pass. The party was a big success and everyone had a good time. I tried to place a call into Woodland so as to reach you at 7:30 but they told me there would be a four hour delay so I cancelled it. I'm sorry that I couldn't do anything for the wedding but it so darn hard to think of anything to say to the, when you don't even know the boy. Be sure and tell me about it.

We have about four more days of school and then we will either ship out to gunnery or get a three day pass and maybe go to advanced. I'm going to the Leake's for Christmas dinner if I'm here.

I passed a twelve word check in Code last Thursday which makes my grade in Code 90% which in turn gives me an overall average of about 95%.

Well I'll let you know what happens.

Jack

52 – Christmas Postcard December 1943

Dear Mother and Dad,

Sure wish I could be there with you to sit at the card table with those big scissors opening up my packages. I can just hear us trying to get Mom out of the kitchen to open her presents. Looking forward to those Kodachromes.

Merry Christmas

Jack

Jack's War – Letters to home from an American WWII Navigator

Christmas Card 1943

Note from Jack's Father:

Attempted to phone Jack today- Talked to Elizabeth Leake- Jack had just left and learned he is O. K. and had Christmas dinner with Elizabeth and Chauncy. Beth and Jane talked to Claude. Bill Sandrose and I were at the hospital. Dad

53 – December 27th, 1943
Group 25, AFPS
Navigator Wing
Ellington Field Texas
    Dear Mother and Dad,

Just received your letter on the wedding which was a perfect description; I almost felt I was there. I hope the people didn't get tired of seeing me in the study. Where was Toots during the wedding? Who all was at the wedding?

The Gods have really smiled on me at last for I'm going to advanced right here at Ellington. In fact, we moved across the field today. I'm two Barrack's away from Linn Wilson which is just like old times. They aren't giving us a minute rest for we start classes tomorrow.

I spent a very amazing Christmas. I had Christmas dinner at the Leake's with four others Doctor Couples who have emigrated from California.

Doctor Peoples who is rather a young and ready wit, Dr. Ogden who is in with Dr. Leake at University of Texas, a Dr. Marquis who was at Stanford but is now on his way to "Duke". We had a big turkey dinner and afterwards two little girls of Dr. Ogden's did a ballet dance and then they showed some Kodachromes of the Leake's trip to Yosemite which was really marvelous (I'm looking forward to your Kodachromes, (they haven't arrived yet). Chauncey and Wilson were there and are really growing up.

I returned to Houston that night with Dr. Ogden and his wife (he is at Baylor) and located a friend and we went in search of rooms, but there were absolutely no rooms to be had. We found one place "Star of Faith Mission". We went in to see what the beds were like and someone shouted "Hallelujah Brother come in and have a plate beans". Needless to say we retreated to the street. We finally found a friend who had a hotel room so we took the top mattress and put it on the floor and slept like logs. The next day we went to the Episcopalian Church, and the fellow I was with said that he thought he knew the Reverend so we went back and sure enough he did. He was very nice and invited us to lunch he reached in his closet to get his coat and he turned out to be a Major (chaplain) in the Army. When we got to his house he immediately

Jack's War – Letters to home from an American WWII Navigator

started talking football and pouring us glasses of wine. When he found out that I was from California he pulled out some California wine and poured us some more. We sat down to another huge turkey dinner. After we finished we tuned in on the Redskins and Bears game and listened to that. He then called up two girls and got us dates and we went sightseeing in his station wagon. Later we took the girls to a show in their car and just made it back to camp in time.

Well we start Classes tomorrow so I'll go to bed.

Jack

Thanks for the short sorter, I'll probably need it.

Also those almonds and walnuts were really appreciated. The guys really go for them.

Jack December 1943 Navigator School age 20

Jack Dec. 1943 Ellington Field Texas

54 – January 2nd, 1944
Class 44-6 Box 2072
Advanced Navigation School
Ellington Field Texas

Dear Mother and Dad,

Here's my first letter of 1944 and I'm writing it from my own desk which is a big modern dark green one. We all have big desks and they are full of navigator equipment which has been issued to us. Our first week has been rough to say the least, and I can see that the seventeen remaining ones are going to be harder yet. You might say we asleep nine and a half hours and work fourteen and a half hours. We are now getting the fundamentals of Navigation so we can use them when we fly. We are supposed to start flying next weekend, but due to the weather I doubt we will fly until the following weekend. We inspected the plane on Friday and they sure are big and powerful. They are a modification of the Lockheed A29 (2 motored). They cruise at about 200mph.

This is an average day schedule

6:45 we get up

7:00 Breakfast clean up shave

8:00-12:00 Navigation

12:00 to 1:00 eat and read mail

1:00-1:30 military period usually drill

1:30-4:30 Navigation

4:30-5:00 Physical Training

5:00 to 7:00 Eat and free time

7:30-9:30 Navigation

Jack's War – Letters to home from an American WWII Navigator

10:00 to 6:45 Sleep

Navigation is just one course but we get four hours of Meteorology a week and about an hour of Code. With all this work we also get some benefits which is mainly the attitude of the officers and instructors. Instead of treating us like Boy Scouts they put the trivial things aside and seem to want to teach us Navigation which is alright with us.

Your description of the wedding was really marvelous. It made me feel as though I was right there. I received the picture of the dollar bill and thank you very much. The Kodachromes have not arrived yet, but I guess they are on their way.

Be sure to give the Democrat my new address (the one on the outside). Well I have to write some other letters so I'll close. Hoping to hear from you and <u>MOTHER</u> soon.

Jack

55 – January 7th, 1944
Class 44-6 Box 2072
Advanced Navigation School
Ellington Field Texas
      Dear Mother and Dad,

This is the first chance I have had all week to write a letter. I've never been so busy in all my life. You should have seen us yesterday when they told us we would fly today (we didn't, it rained). This flight will be our pilotage mission. This is a type of navigation based on reference points on the ground which you locate on your maps. Well anyway we had maps all over the desks, and we were practically climbing the walls to plot our courses.

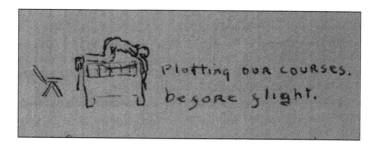

Enthusiastic Navigational planning

We refer to the "sectionals" when doing Pilotage for they have all the cultural and relief features on them. There are four legs to this mission and we each take a leg. This is our approximate course: Ellington to Beeville Tex, to Bryan Tex, to Many La, back to Ellington. It might sound simple but we are busy every minute of the time figuring how far we have gone and just where we are and when to the exact minute we will arrive at our destination. We sit up there right by the pilot and when we cross a railroad or fly over a town we check it on the maps and with two or three check points you can estimate or approximate your track over the ground or correct your heading so as to hit your destination right on the nose. I think we will fly tomorrow or Sunday. We do all our figuring on a "E6b" computer which is based on the same principle as a slide rule only you can do "anything" you'll ever need to do on it. It is the most amazing thing I've ever seen.

I received the Kodachromes yesterday and I have never been so homesick in all my life. Everybody was crowded around me as I sat back with my feet on my desk with the little projector at my eye reaching over sticking in a new picture in every minute. Boy! It was just like coming home. Those were some pictures. You should have seen those New Yorkers "Oh and Ah" when they saw Mom's gardens and flowers. When I showed them the one of you at your desk, Dad, they said he sure looks like a doctor. I can see why Jane married Claude. "Wow" what a handsome guy, just like Gary Cooper.

Jack's War – Letters to home from an American WWII Navigator

I guess my Christmas present to you will be coming along any time now, at least I hope so.

I've received a book from Aunt Katherine and a box of candy from Aunt Grace and I don't have Aunt Harriet and Aunt Bessie's address and they sent me a dollar and I also don't have Uncle Renny's. But I absolutely don't have time to write letters, and I would appreciate if you would inform them that I'm very thankful and will write just as soon as I have time. Tell Jane and Claude to "hang on" to that, I received their box of candy and money order for $5 and I will write just as soon as I can. Here we go again.

Jack

Write lots of letters for this is our only relaxation the whole day.

56 – January 13th, 1944
Class 44-6 Box 2072
Advanced Navigation School
Ellington Field Texas
          Dear Mother and Dad,

Just a note to let you know that I am still fighting the civil war and still in Navigation School although we had what they call a faze exam which covered all the material we had up to date and it lasted three and a half hours. It was just like a college final except it didn't have any material that we hadn't covered and they didn't have any trick questions, just the straight stuff we need to know and nothing else.

I guess you didn't hear about our first mission yet but boy it was some flight. To say we were busy every minute is "triumph of understatement" (to coin a phrase).

We took off while I was fixing my maps and I didn't even know it. When I looked out that window there we were right over our departure and from then on, in fact for 680 miles, I was "pin pointing" myself on the map figuring our Ground Speed, Plotting our track over the ground, getting an Estimated time of Arrival for destination, calling the pilot on the interphone, taking a double drift and before I knew it we were back at Ellington Field. I passed okay but boy I've really got to get on the ball and learn to work in the air. It is a lot different than on the ground. Our next mission is to Calibrate our Compass (an explanation would fill three of these sheets) and Calibrate our airspeed meters. This mission is going to be plenty tough for we do a thousand turns and while working mentally at the same time, it makes you sick.

I sure would like you to come down Mother, but I just don't know if I"ll graduate and if I did it would seem silly to come all the way down to Texas just for that. I think I get ten days travelling time if I do graduate, and then I'' be right home. You would no sooner get here, and we would have to turn around and go right back, but we can wait and see.

I sure am enjoying the Kodachromes and you ought to see the fellows wander over and pick up a few and then start right through the whole pack wanting to know who each person is and if those oranges really grew in our back yard and how old is my sister.

Say Mother, would you thank Mrs Griffith for those stuffed prunes for me. They sure were good.

Mother, I am not sore and anybody yet, but will you please hint to A.K and A. G. (Aunts Katherine and Grace) when they write me a letter to please not give me moral lectures on what to watch out for in the army, or I hope you don't drink like the other army men do. Good gosh, I'm not ten years old anymore. I know what the army is like and I know what kind of girl I like and that nothing anybody tells me is going to change my mind on what is right and what is wrong. Please do this, for you know I hate lectures.

Thanks for all the letters lately. They sure do brighten up the day.

Jack

P.S. Say hello to Toots, glad she is better.

57 – January 23rd, 1944
Class 44-6 Box 2072
Advanced Navigation School
Ellington Field Texas
Dear Mother and Dad,

Another week of navigation has passed and it feels like they just poured a year's course into us. About Thursday we started planning for our third mission which was a precision Dead Reckoning. This means maintaining a desired direction by reading your instruments. We flew up into North Texas to an initial point where we turned off into the supposed target which was an airfield. I had the return leg and had fair results. I hit my initial point on the nose but my Estimated Time of Arrival was off by four minutes. The whole trip took four hours but we never even noticed it. We are working every minute in the air, and then don't even have time to do everything we should.

Say I sure could use that watch if you don't need it up there. They are supposed to issue us one, but I doubt we will get one for a couple of months.

Sorry to hear Claude is moving, but that is typical of the breaks in the army. I sure hope you take care of Koli and get a little fat on him for when I come home this spring I have a little score to settle with him.

Say hello to Toots

Jack

58 – January 27th, 1944
Class 44-6 Box 2072
Advanced Navigation School
Ellington Field Texas
Dear Mother and Dad,

We aren't having classes tonight so I'd thought I'd drop you a line. Most of our flight flew their second D.R. (Dead Reckoning) mission but there weren't enough planes so we will probably fly ours Saturday morning. It is our first chance to direct the ships by instruments and you can imagine the suspense as you walk up to the front of the ship to see if you have hit your destination and if your E.T.A. is on the nose. As I told you in my last letter we have already flown one DR mission and I did just so so.

We started celestial yesterday and boy! I can see where that is going to give us plenty of trouble. We know about twenty five stars in sky above us and it wasn't hard to learn but that is just a minor point in celestial. We are beginning to get the little intricacies which make navigation the art it is. Sometimes they give us a problem such as taking off at a certain time and to control the groundspeed so as to reach destination at the precise minute and to figure our gas consumption and to know how many fuel hours we have left on five minutes before we reach our target to notify the pilot how many feet/min to drop so as to be at a certain attitude. It is all very interesting, but it sure is hard to remember all they teach us.

Jack's War – Letters to home from an American WWII Navigator

I received the three new Kodachromes and enjoyed them. Seeing Mr Peart and your diagram in your letter reminds me of those three very colourful days at the Peart ranch. Say hello for me and tell him my teeth are still razor sharp.

That camping trip sure sounds swell to me. There is nothing I would rather do than just go look at a Pine covered mountain or drag a fly over a stream. Where do you think we ought to go? Most of the streams will be pretty high and muddy due to the snow but we're going any way even if we don't catch one little fish.

Received a nice letter from Claude today I guess they have left for Camp Edwards by now. Is Jane quitting her job for good or just the three weeks? I think she ought to keep working out there, it seems like such a good deal. I could still use that watch to a good advantage if you could spare it. Well I have to go to bed so-

Jack

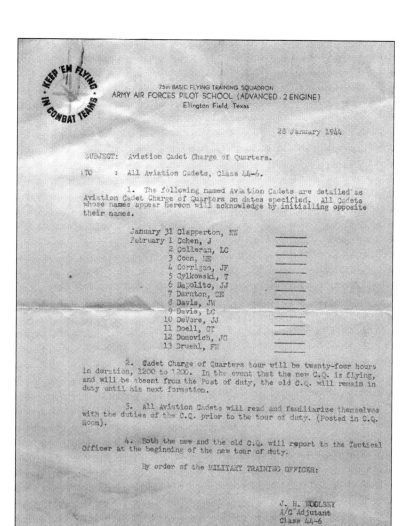

Assignments from Jack

Jack's War – Letters to home from an American WWII Navigator

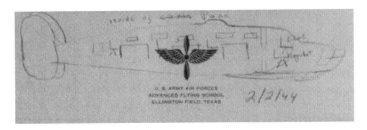

Plane Diagram

59 – February 2nd, 1944
Class 44-6 Box 2072
Advanced Navigation School
Ellington Field Texas

    Dear Mother and Dad,

    Here is a diagram of the plane at the top of letter.

    Just received the nuts and dads letter from the Chancellor. I have also received the raft book and thank you for all.

    My last two days have really been busy ones. We flew both days and they were long flights. On Monday we flew over to Mc Comb Mississippi and back. I guess I'm one of the few guys that have been east of the Mississippi but never touched ground. Tuesday we flew our first "Dog leg" DR mission I will explain this to you later right now I'm going to try to give you an idea of what the four navigators do on these missions. Each mission is divided up into two legs (out and back). There are only three cabin seats to work at, so naturally one of us has to ride up in the co-pilot seat and do "Pilotage". You can also see that the other three navigators can't all direct the pilot because all their readings differ, so one fellow directs the pilot and the other two do what they call "Follow the Pilot". In every combat squadron there is a squadron navigator who is the only one directing the planes in formation the rest do "Follow the Pilot" so you can see we get practise at all duties. Now the difference between "Direct the Pilot" and "Follow the Pilot" is that the one going D to P has a true course to make good and he makes his compass read what it should by having the Pilot correct three or four degrees left or right (example wind drift). He assumes that he is on the course that he plotted. The others doing F the P read their compass every five minutes and take an average when they go to plot their position, they never correct to make their compasses read right they just follow the Pilot. This is merely a check on the first navigator and also if he is disabled in any way, they know right where they are and can immediately take over, and start directing the Pilot. This may seem a little hazy but maybe this will clean it up. The one doing D to P maybe didn't get the right instrumental readings and is actually off course, well the one doing F the P will know this and have his position plotted exactly where he is. This dog leg we flew yesterday was hard because we had to turn at certain coordinates which couldn't be determined by landmarks so if you didn't DR right to it you can see what would happen.

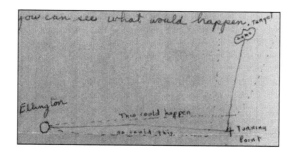

Navigation diagram

Well I guess you've had enough navigation for today. Class dismissed.

Jack

60 – February 9th, 1944
Class 44-6 Box 2072
Advanced Navigation School
Ellington Field Texas

Dear Mother and Dad,

Well how are things going on the home front? Your letter arrived today with the Kodachromes and half the class came over to see them. They all remarked that Mom was sure good looking and had beautiful hair. That is one where she is holding the pups, boy they are sure cute. I hope you don't give them away because Jane is coming home to live.

I asked my teacher if he knew Mr Thatcher and he said yes, his name is Lt. Smidderko.

We were issued our watches yesterday so I won't need that one of yours. I flew last Friday and hit the target right on the nose but was a minute and half off on my E.T.A. but all in all it was a very successful mission. We are now about 2 weeks ahead on flying time so we are laying off.

We are getting celestial now and it is really too complicated to explain, but the general idea is that we take the altitude of three stars, preferably about 60 degrees apart.

The circles represent the places on the earth where you could obtain that certain altitude for that star. Where the three circles cross is what they call a fix and that is where you are.

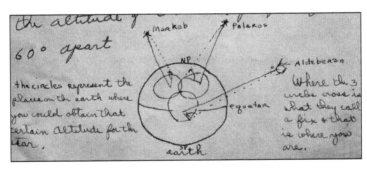

The Fix in navigation

This week we are having classes on Saturday and Sunday which doesn't set too well with us but you can't do anything about it even if you knew Hap Arnold. Well I can't think of any more news just now. I sure do wish mother would sit down sometimes like Sunday night and write a nice long letter when she isn't rushed.

Jack

P.S. will send the Kodachromes back. This money order letter will be kept on hand (in this house where I can lay my hands on it) in case I graduate and need money to buy clothes.

61 – February 18th, 1944
Class 44-6 Box 2072
Advanced Navigation School
Ellington Field Texas
Dear Mother and Dad,

Still at the old grind but we are going to fly tomorrow so that will be relieve the monotony. We have been studying about Radio Navigation this past week and it is very interesting so I'm going to give you a rough idea how we determine our position by Radio. Air Planes are equipped with what call a Radio Compass this is worked by a "loop" on top of the plane which received radio waves and turns so as to receive them which in turn, turns our Radio Compass in the cabin and gives us the angle between the heading of our ship and the Radio station which is sending out waves.

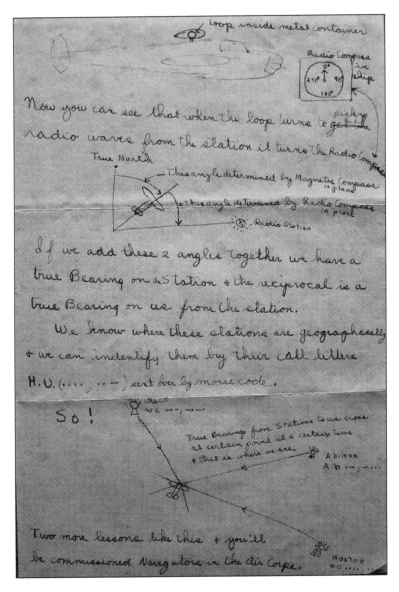

Radio compass diagrams

Now you can see that when the loop turns to pick up radio waves from the station it turns the Radio Compass.

If we add these two angles together we have a true Bearing on the station and the reciprocal is a true bearing on us from the station. We know where these stations are geographically and we can identify them buy their call letters H.U (...,.._) sent over by Morse code. So! True bearings from stations to us cross at a certain point at a certain time and that is where we are.

Two more lessons like this and you'll be commissioned Navigators in the Air Corps.

We had a ground mission last night that was a humdinger and I didn't stop working once for two and a half hours. We started out on a parallel search. On our last leg we supposedly received a radio message to find a ship at certain position so we went to the spot where it was last seen and started an expanding square search until we sighted the vessel. We then were told we had fifteen minutes of gas left and to designate which airport to fly to.

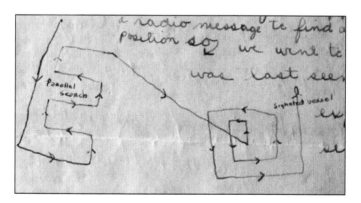

Ground mission path

Tomorrow we are going out over the gulf and actually fly this search and it will be plenty tough for the legs are so short that you don't have time to work ahead to determine when to turn, but I guess it'll work out okay.

I received the Kodachromes and really enjoyed them. Jane and Claude sure do have a cute house. I am sending the

Jack's War – Letters to home from an American WWII Navigator

Kodachromes back today and hope they reach you in time. I didn't realize it was so imperative that they be sent so soon.

Glad to hear that Koli is looking better and that Toots has accepted the pups. I kept a couple of the slides to look at but will send them on as you send them to me. Well I've got to get studying so---.

Jack

62 – February 25th, 1944
Class 44-6 Box 2072
Advanced Navigation School
Ellington Field Texas
Dear Mother and Dad,

I have missed your letters this week but probably will get them tomorrow I hope. We haven't been doing much but theory this last week, one flight which was practically nothing. The weather has been poor so no flying, and we hear that we won't fly for another two weeks due to everybody being behind schedule. The one flight we did make was swinging the astrocompass by using the sun which is too difficult to explain, but the astrocompass is used to determine the magnetic disturbances set up in the plane by bomb loads, and permanent magnetism of the soft iron. Anyway it was a very beautiful ride for we flew just above some cumulus clouds which are very beautiful. It was just like looking over an ocean of white capes hundreds of feet high.

I sure do enjoy the Democrat now; besides hearing about my friends in the service, I am getting a great kick out of this question that Mrs Mc Ghee has brought up and kicked around till all the clubs have taken it up. I am glad to see she is ducking the issue now for she could be blasted right out of point if asked what restrictions she put on her own daughter when she was in high school. I think this thing has been coming up for a long time and it was just coming to a head when I left high school. Dad will remember hardly any of the fellows would train for football or basketball and would never study on school nights. I really appreciate your restrictions on me now, but I think this curfew law would be about as poor as anything they could suggest. I think Mr Harper is the only one on the right track. You see very few have homes to go home to like Bob Griffith, Jim Harper and I, where we can sit down by a fire listen to good music or read a book and even have a coke. I know you realize this but what I'm driving at is that sending a kid home to a one room madhouse is just as bad as leaving him on the streets. He would soon grow to hate his home and naturally would sneak out and hit for Sacramento at the first opportunity. Well the thing I would do it for you men like Luther De Bois, Mr Crawford etc. who can get things done and not make statements to the Democrat get together and see what you could do for the fellows to make them appreciate the finer things while growing up and give them a place to do this in. Well my idea would be something like a service club on the army fields today. Not some dinky little scout cabin but something on a big scale. Woodland really needs something like this for there is absolutely nothing to do there. I would suggest a large reading room with hundreds of magazines, good books and some good classical music which you can absorb while reading; you'd be surprised how one can learn to like it that way instead of having it shoved down their throat. Also, have a big dancing floor so the weekends would be fun and they could dance in the afternoon to a juke box. This is a bit fantastic I guess, but I would also have a bowling alley and a room for ping pong and pool. This would be a place for every kid in town to come to with no restrictions to race or social class. If I had it my way I would serve beer to the older boys just to show them that they weren't being treated like babies, but anyway have a fountain in the place too. And by all means, let them handle their own conduct rules by appointing committee for this and that whatever is needed. **No** chaperones or onlooking parents that would scare half of them

Jack's War – Letters to home from an American WWII Navigator

away. Also a little entertainment of Friday or Saturday night would help. Something like this backed up by you people with an organized outdoor athletic program being constructed by the YMCA and the Boy Scouts would never give the kids a chance to think about anything else and would thus clean up the problem which is being kicked around in the paper so adequately. I realize some things would take quite a bit of money to launch, but if it could be done it would pay back a million times its cost in producing good all-around fellows instead of the "wise guys" who know it all. Also you see a lot of people sending their children back to night school instead of private ones. Well their goes taps and so I'll hit the sack.

Jack

63 – March 4th, 1944
Class 44-6 Box 2072
Advanced Navigation School
Ellington Field Texas
            Dear Mother and Dad,

        Received all your letters and packages up to date. The nuts arrived in good order and were devoured within two days with several requests for the formula to the sugared nuts. I sure do want that sweater, so send it on down and I'll wear it on my flight missions. So its storming in California, well the weather is rather different down here. It's sultry and hot with clouds hanging over the field most of the time. We aren't flying at all but they have been pouring the theory down our throats ten hours a day and consequently we have covered just about everything the course requires so the rest of our time will be taken up with flying and problems. We have taken up a new method of plotting Celestial and Radio navigation which is similar to the British system and I think it is very good. We are the 2nd Class to take up this method. Celestial Navigation is extremely interesting and brings up many questions in your mind which is actually fun to discuss with your friends. Last night the fellows told me I was talking about stars and the sun in my sleep. Oh yes, I received <u>Eneas Africanus</u> and still enjoy it I remembered it from the Readers Digest. Finn Walker is still here and graduates three weeks before I do. The fellows in my element are all from New York; one from Brooklyn, one from the Bronx and the other from New York. They are very typical of N.Y. especially the one from Brooklyn.

Glad to hear that Koli is looking better and that you are feeding Star up. I can just see toots looking up begging to go out to the barn. I can't wait to get home and see her and all of you. I didn't forget Jane's birthday so you can quit worrying. I also received a big box of cookies from her and Claude which the whole flight enjoyed. That sure is swell about the "B" basketball team, if you see Coach Bailey congratulate him for me. Well, have to go so.

Jack

64 – March 12th, 1944
Class 44-6 Box 2072
Advanced Navigation School
Ellington Field Texas
Dear Mother and Dad,

It's Monday night and I guess it's been a long time since I last wrote you, but it's been kind of hard to think of anything to say for we haven't been in an airplane for weeks because of the weather and the graduating classes have the priorities. We are really going to have a lot of flying to do when we start, and that will be the real test of whether we are navigators or not. We have completed practically all ground work except for the odds and ends, and I have done average so far. If I do make the grade I'm thinking seriously of flying home if possible. It will shorten the trip by a day and a half I think and boy! I sure am anxious to see you all. Every night it takes me about a half an hour to go to sleep just thinking how the house and how everything will look. I can just see Toots

Jack's War – Letters to home from an American WWII Navigator

come running around the house with her nose all wriggled up and her tail wagging back and forth. We have seven more weeks to go but it seems like seven years but I guess the time will finally roll around. That sure is swell about Claude still being around and getting his Sergeant's stripes. I must be nice to have them up on the weekends. I wish I could be there to enjoy them. By the way Mom, the sweater came today and it's really swell and fits perfect. I'll use it on my night flights to keep warm, and it will still give me plenty of freedom of my arms so I can do my plotting. You might be interested in the way we learn our stars. There are really very few Navigation stars but we learn them by constellation such as the Big Dipper, Belt of Orion, the Seven Sisters, square of Pegasus and such. Take a look at the Big Dipper sometime early at night it looks one way and different in the morning.

Well I'll have to go out and practice with my sextant before going to bed so.

Jack

65 – March 19th, 1944
Class 44-6 Box 2072
Advanced Navigation School
Ellington Field Texas
Dear Mother and Dad,

It is Sunday morning and we are standing by to see if we are going to fly one of our search missions. I doubt if we will for it is pretty cloudy at the present moment. We still haven't been up in the air for a long time due to the new system of using the planes. About our last three weeks we have all the places and will probably go on what they call detached service. We will take off and land at another field and stay out for a couple of days and get in a lot of flying time. That is interesting what Dr Foote said about it being hard to hit Wake Island, but it isn't because we can't read "drift" off the water it is just hard to fly that for and hit a pin point like a small Island.

Heard from Pete Watts the other day and he is up in Oregon flying P39's and is about ready to come down to Los Angeles and start training in P38's. Glad to hear Star is picking up and Toots is feeling fine. Well there isn't any more news.

Jack

66 – March 26th, 1944
Class 44-6 Box 2072
Advanced Navigation School
Ellington Field Texas
Dear Mother and Dad,

Another week has passed and five more to go. This past week has been rather rugged, in fact we had two tough flight missions. They were both searches that really keep you on your toes as far as navigation is concerned. Both flights lasted six and a half hours and you would be amazed how tired one can get just sitting up there navigating. The first flight was a parallel search which goes like this:

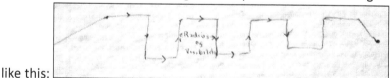

Parallel Search

The second one was a sector search which goes like this.

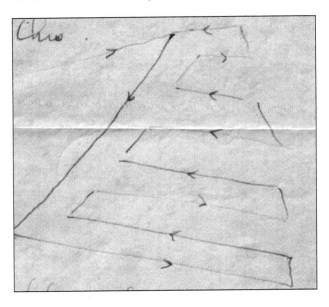

Sector Search

The reason we fly these searches is that it is the best practice for DR. we can get. I was directing the sector search and we flew right over the Mississippi River. When we ended up I was only three miles left of where we should be and supposedly that is pretty fair Navigation. We covered about 1100 miles in all on the sector search.

I received the nuts Saturday and sure do appreciate them. Say hello to Jane and Claude for me. I can't seem to sit down and write anymore I don't know why maybe I'm just in a "batting slump". I sure could use a flashlight for these coming Celestial missions. Also, if you can get a hold of some V120 film I think I can get some snap shots of what is going on down here. Well that's all for now.

Jack

67 – April 1st, 1944
Class 44-6 Box 2072
Advanced Navigation School
Ellington Field Texas

Dear Mother and Dad,

Saturday afternoon and again we have classes. This is getting to be regular routine, loaf through the week and work like hell on the weekends. I think last night was my most exciting night I've spent since entering the Air Corps. We were given a route from Ellington to Enid, Oklahoma and told to be ready to fly our first celestial mission: Well we drew our route in and got all ready and marched down to the flight line. I always seem to worry before each flight, and no matter how many times I've done it I always wonder if I'll be able to do it when we get up there 10,000 in the air. We took off just at dusk and it was really perfect flying. Pretty soon the sky darkened and the Navigation stars began to smile on young J.H.W. Well got out my trusty sextant and fired quickly at three stars and worked them out. It still amazes me that with this use of a sextant and some tables you can place yourself within ten miles of your actual position. Well everything worked out pretty well and we circled Enid and started back. I was doing night pilotage coming back and that means setting up there in the co-pilots seat and checking the towns as we go by, all you see of the towns is their lights but they presents a pattern which you see on your map and locate yourself pretty readily. We went right over Oklahoma City and also passed over Dallas which helped locate myself. The flight doesn't really amount to much as a whole but you see we have been preparing and preparing for night flights and when it goes so smoothly it just makes you feel good.

Linn Wilson graduates this next week and he is Wing Commander of all Navigation and will undoubtedly win the military award which he rightly deserves. He almost flew out to Sacramento on detached service and was all prepared to phone to you (notice Mom I didn't say "phone up") Thank Jane and Claude for the box of candy for I sure do appreciate it. Please inform the relatives that I'm

Jack's War – Letters to home from an American WWII Navigator

extremely busy at this time and will write after "if" I graduate. I sure do think that is a good idea about Koli and agree with Jane's method of Training. Thanks for the Cal Monthly and green sheets. Well here we go again so.

Jack

Oh I forgot to tell you that I think it's grand that Jane is having a baby.

68 – April 7th, 1944
Class 44-6 Box 2072
Advanced Navigation School
Ellington Field Texas
          Dear Mother and Dad,

Well we are really on the home stretch now, and the way they are pouring the stuff at us it really feels like it.

Linn Wilson graduated this weekend and Linn walked off with the military award. You should see him in his uniform. Boy, he looks like a million dollars. His mother and brother and step-father came down to see him and took the three of us (Hugh White is the other boy who has been with us since Texas Tech) to the Empire Room at the largest hotel in Houston and treated us to a real banquet with wine and all the trimmings. Linn had his girlfriend and I took Linn's cousin who is a blond beauty. Boy we sure did have a marvellous time.

Linn is going to Lincoln Nebraska to train in flying forts. The boys who are outstanding in Navigation go to Roswell New Mexico to take a six week course in Bombardiering from which they are

110

either assigned to the big B29s, or the medium bombers. Don't worry about me though, for I am far from being outstanding. I'm just an average navigator. Our celestial missions are the most fun for me because you work entirely by the stars and a chart and are never see the ground then you tell the pilot the estimated time of arrival (ETA) and sure enough there in front of you looms the town that is your target.

There is very little news so,

Jack

Here is a small diagram depicting our work:

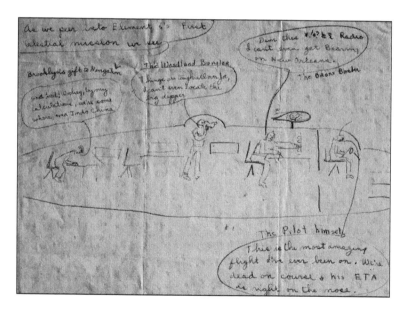

Navigation methods

Jack's War – Letters to home from an American WWII Navigator

69 – April 11th, 1944
Class 44-6 Box 2072
Advanced Navigation School
Ellington Field Texas
     Dear Mother and Dad,

Just came back from a supposedly long flight but the airplane I was in had to make an emergency landing due to a bad motor and we spent the night at the field we landed at.

We came back the next day and an official notice was on the board that we will graduate a week earlier due to the new system they are putting into effect here at Ellington, and this means we will be flying up to the last minute. I hope I will be able to leave the field April 22nd and come home on the train. This sort of messes up my train reservations but don't worry I'm coming home if I have to walk. Well nothing new but I'll be flying practically all the time.

    Jack

70 – April 12th, 1944
Class 44-6 Box 2072
Advanced Navigation School
Ellington Field Texas

    Dear Mother,

Still flying every day and busy getting ready to graduate. Spent two days at Scott Field, Illinois on detached service. Got into St. Louis in our big leather flying jackets and we sure did have fun. But Oh! The next morning when I had to navigate the plane I was really sick after about 800 miles and the last 400, well I just did get by.

Your plans are okay theoretically but remember I'm still in the army. I have no reservations on the train due to a change in graduation and I'm not sure I'll get furlough or whether I'll leave Saturday night or Sunday. I suggest you wait till I get to Los Angeles or Riverside and let me phone you.

Send me a telegram as to your whereabouts and your telephone number. Jane writes from one address and you the other. Well don't worry, I'll get hold of you when I get to L.A. or Riverside.

Jack

Chapter 6

Graduation from Ellington Navigation School

April 22nd, 1944
Class 44-6 Box 2072
Advanced Navigation School
Ellington Field Texas

Leather bound Graduation Invitation

The Air Forces Advanced Navigation School

of

Ellington Field, Texas

announces the graduation of

Class 44-6

Saturday morning, April twenty-second

nineteen hundred and forty-four

at nine o'clock

Post Theatre

Graduation April 22nd 1944

John H. Woolsey

Lieutenant, Air Corps
Army of the United States

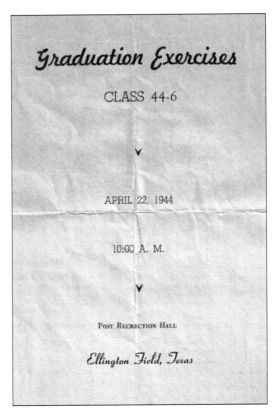

Graduation Program

ARMY AIR FORCES ADVANCED NAVIGATION SCHOOL

ELLINGTON FIELD, TEXAS

R. C. ROCKWOOD

Colonel, Air Corps
Commanding Officer

WILLIAM S. BOWEN

Major, Air Corps
Group Commander

WINCELL R. CHADY	**JOHN MELIUS**	**CHARLES A. STEEN**
Major, Air Corps	*Captain, Air Corps*	*Captain, Air Corps*
Squadron Commander	*Dir. of Nav. Tng.*	*Director of Flying*

R. H. MARTIN

Captain, Air Corps
School Secretary

PHILIP H. HILL

Lieutenant, Air Corps
Class Commander
Military

JOHN A. O'DONOHUE

Lieutenant, Air Corps
Class Commander
Navigation

AVIATION CADET DETACHMENT CADET OFFICERS

WING COMMANDER
Isaacks, J. D.

WING EXECUTIVE
Krakower, J. D.

GROUP COMMANDER
O'Brien, E. J.

GROUP COMMANDER
Geary, J. W.

Graduation Commanders

Graduation Exercises

CLASS 44-6

Post Recreation Hall

ELLINGTON FIELD, TEXAS

APRIL 22, 1944

10:00 A. M.

MARCH . . . . *Ellington Field Band*

AIR CORPS SONG . . . . *Ellington Field Band*

INVOCATION . . . . *Chaplain*

OATHS OF OFFICE . . . . *Secretary*

PRESENTATION OF AWARDS . . . . . . *Commandant of Cadets*

GRADUATION ADDRESS

PRESENTATION OF WINGS AND LETTERS OF APPOINTMENT

BENEDICTION . . . . *Chaplain*

NATIONAL ANTHEM . . . . *Entire Assembly*

Graduation Program

A letter from Jacks parent's friend Mrs Leake who lives near Houston Tx.

Dear Beth and Homer:-

I went to the graduation exercises this A.M. You certainly can be proud of Jack. I think he is the sweetest thing I ever knew. He thanked me three times for coming and appeared so pleased to see me.

I had but ten minutes with him after the exercises. He has been working so hard, and I could see he has lost some weight. Somehow- maybe it was just my mood-but he looked just like the little boy Jack to me again. He certainly is fine looking and among the tallest and strongest there. Really, I was terribly touched, but he didn't know it.

In fact I think I had quite an emotional jag thinking of you both all the miles as I drove up and how strange events had placed us down here, and that I had the privilege of representing "the family back home" for Jack.

About one hundred fifty boys graduated, I would judge and around the same number of guests. Seemed mostly young wives and sweethearts to me but again, perhaps it was my mood as I looked at so much glorious youth.

What a band they had. Honestly, Sousa in his day didn't approach them. It was marvellous. The speech was only eight minutes and up on discipline. I know those boys have been working. I hope Jack can get down here before further orders. He didn't have such as yet but presume he does now. He rather hoped to be sent to Roswell to school and made me feel good by telling me that he would see Chauncey immediately.

Jack's War – Letters to home from an American WWII Navigator

I'll enclose the program in case you don't have one for the scrapbook. I keep such of Chauncey's letters which are spelled "Dear Mable of Old"

Jack phoned me of the change of date and I do think it was so thoughtful of him. I can' get over how marvellous he is and what a real man to have developed from the little five year old I knew. I wish he could have leave to see you all.

I told Chauncey that I felt I was back in the U.S. again as all the names were so American and not a double name nor a Jr. among them. Every man on his own feet. Really it is a spectacle and your son John the best representative there.

Wilson would have gone but his R.B.C.s flared higher and Dr Stone was out of Galveston and we couldn't ask permission. He won't budge without Dr Stone's sanction. Jack asked so kindly about him and did seem to miss him. Really I have never talked to anyone who seemed to ring all the tight bells just at the right time and correct degree as your son Jack.

All Love

Elizabeth (Leake)

Western Union Telegrams:

*APR. 19 1944 FROM JACK TO HIS FATHER DR JOHN H WOOLSEY

HAVE 10 HOURS FLYING LEFT. WILL GRADUATE BUT MAY HAVE TO REMAIN AND FLY. CAN'T MAKE DEFINITE STATEMENT AS TO ARRIVAL AT RIVERSIDE WILL WIRE WHEN DEFINITE.

JOHN

*APR 22 1944 FROM JACK TO MOTHER MRS JOHN H WOOLSEY (MOTHER)

GRADUATED, UNASSIGNED AS YET, REMAIN AT ELLINGTON TILL MONDAY

JOHN

*APR 24TH 1944 FROM JACK TO MRS JOHN H WOOLSEY (MOTHER)

NO ORDERS TODAY JUST SITTING TIGHT SEE YOU SOON.

JOHN

*APR 26TH 1944 FROM JACK TO MRS JOHN H WOOLSEY (MOTHER)

STILL COOLING OUR HEELS IT LOOKS LIKE THEY MIGHT COME IN SAT FLYING TONIGHT AS INSTRUCTOR QUITE A CHANGE

JOHN

* APR 27TH 1944 FROM DR JOHN H WOOLSEY TO MRS JOHN H WOOLSEY

NO WORD FROM JACK. HAVE YOU? WISH TO MAKE PLANS

HOMER

*APR 29TH 1944 FROM JACK TO MRS JOHN H WOOLSEY (MOTHER)

ON WAY TO RIVERSIDE .GET THERE SOMETIME SUNDAY NIGHT REPORT TO LINCOLN MAY 12

JACK

*APR 30TH 1944 FROM JACK TO MRS JOHN H WOOLSEY (MOTHER)

TRY MEET ME SAN BERNADINO ETA 1200 PM

JACK

Graduation Magazine Cover April 1944

Jack's Picture in the Astro-dome

April 28th 1944

<u>Woodland Democrat</u>

"Our Boys" column

Jack Woolsey Is New Lieutenant

Second lieutenant John H. (Jack) Woolsey, son of Dr and Mrs J. H. Woolsey has received is silver wings and been commissioned as a navigator in the army air forces.

Jack's War – Letters to home from an American WWII Navigator

Lieutenant Woolsey was graduated from the navigation filed at Ellington Field, Texas. He has spent the last six months at Ellington learning all types of aerial direction, including radio, celestial observation and flying by landmarks.

He will be granted a short leave and then be assigned to tactical unit or combat crew for final preparation for actual combat within a few weeks.

Woodland Democrat

Woolsey Going To Nebraska

Enjoying his visit here with his parents Dr and Mrs John Homer Woolsey,

And scores of friends is Second Lieutenant John H. "Jack" Woolsey, who reports to Lincoln Nebraska May 12. The flyer, a navigator in a B24 Liberator, expects to be in Berkeley today to say hello to college friends, and to attend the annual California-U.S.C. track meet.

"Jack" was graduated recently from navigation school at Ellington Field, Texas. The next stop in his training will prepare him for actual combat work. He likes his work, and reports he receives excellent training and the best of care and treatments.

He reports Woodland is "really home sweet home" to him after spending is share of time in Texas.

"Jack" never looked better and said flying is a great sport.

Note from Jack's father:Jack home for one week May3rd to 9th -3 days with the horses, two days house and golf, two days at Berkeley, Party on Sunday night –Left may 9th Dad

71 – May 10th, 1944

Ogden Utah

Postcard Description: Latter Day Saints Ogden Utah

Dear Mom and Dad,

Just joined this church after smoking that foul cigar.

Lost all my money in a poker game last night. Trip very uneventful. See you soon it says here.

Jack

72 – May 12th 1944

Chicago Ill

Dear Mom and Dad,

Just pulled into Cheyenne. Trip very good so far. Won all my money back last night. Here goes my train and it has a 50 yard head start.

Jack

73 – May 15th, 1944

Sqd A C&R. P

Lincoln AFB

Lincoln, Nebraska

Dear Mother and Dad,

Sorry for the delay but we have been just sitting around waiting to get an address. Arrived safely and reported to the field the next morning along with about eight hundred other 2nd Lieutenants. We have been standing in lines ever since and getting started on a four day processing. After these four days we are eligible to ship out for different fields here in the middle west where we will start our flying.

These four days consist of combat lectures, shooting the 45 pistol, going through the pressure chamber and first aid lectures

Jack's War – Letters to home from an American WWII Navigator

plus cholera, yellow fever plus typhus shots. Outside of this we don't do much of anything except sleep and eat.

The weather has been rather hot lately, but nothing like Texas. The night I arrived in Lincoln, I stayed at the Cornhusker Hotel and the next day when I left who should be giving a speech but John Bricker Ohio Republican.

I tried to call you yesterday but due to a delay and a formation I had to make, I had to cancel it. I can't believe I had six days at home and it went so fast. It sure was fun. I am pretty sure I'll get another leave before going overseas. I better for this one has just made me more homesick.

Let you know my next move.

Jack

Chapter 7

Lincoln Air Force Base

74 – May 30th, 1944
Sqd A C&R. P
Lincoln AFB
Lincoln Nebraska
Dear Mother and Dad,

Just received Mother's letter which reminded me I hadn't written for a couple of weeks. It is not because I'm busy either but because I have done absolutely nothing for about fourteen days. It's just the same old army as when I was a cadet. In fact I am missing a shipment tomorrow because of my name again. I'm getting used to that now. They sure do a wonderful job of messing things up. They tell us they need navigators so bad that they can't send us to what they call 1st faze training, but have to send us to 2nd and 3rd faze right away. That makes us about the most undertrained man on the ship, but the rub comes when we sit around here seeing these movies we've seen ten times when we could have got that 1st faze training in while we were sitting here. As I go further on in my training I see where the navigator plays a very unimportant role. A very few do the actual navigation. Boy I sure will be glad to get into a combat area where they really mean business and don't dilly dally around.

Have been up to Omaha the last two weekends, and it is really a good town. On our way back this last time the fellow we got a ride with took us through "Boy's Town". It is some place.

That sure is swell about Jane and Claude going to New York. You can burn up my letters if you want but you better go through Dad's first, there might be something I want to keep. No, I didn't

Jack's War – Letters to home from an American WWII Navigator

forget my shoes and caps but you better send that Khaki Officer's hat when I get to my next station.

Just learned that Bob went to Wendover Utah. I could be sent there. Here's hoping. Don't worry if you don't hear from me for it's just because I'm not doing anything

Jack

75 – June 1st, 1944
 Sqd A C&R.P.
Lincoln AFB
Lincoln Nebraska
        Dear Mother and Dad,

Don't like to carry all this money around so I'll send it home and you can invest as you see fit; War Bonds etc.

Jack

P.S. Just got a telegram from Jane and Claude from Omaha. I could have sneaked up there to see them if I had known before.

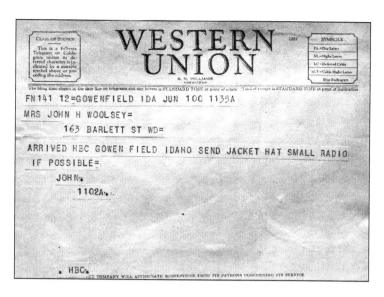

Orders to move to Boise Idaho

76 – Post card from Cheyenne Wyoming

Dear Mom and dad,

Trip fine so far write at Boise.

Jack

77 – June 8th, 1944
4:30 AM
Sqd. A C&R. P
Lincoln AFB
Lincoln Nebraska
 Dear Mother and Dad,

  Just a note to let you know I'm back in circulation again and I am leaving this base this morning. Our destination is Boise Idaho which is good because it is the closest possible I could get to home. Been having quite a time lately having one party right after the other, but I am glad to get back to work. Was up to Omaha last weekend and had my usual good time. I have a girl up there that I take out.

I met Geneva Lockridge (Maiden name) Hughes (first marriage) Osbourne (her present husband) in front of the Cornhusker the other night with her husband Lt. Osbourne who is a navigator just home from England. I used to go to school with Geneva and she knows you dad, and as usual won't have any other doctor. Had dinner with them and he gave me some good tips on combat.

Visited the capital here in Lincoln the other night and ran into a janitor cleaning the governor's rooms. He took me in and what a place. Wow. I sat right down in the Gov's chair and passed a few laws myself. They really have a beautiful capital.

The weather is really unusually hot, just right, cold and raining cats and dogs right now.

Nebraska is very nice, rolling hills, fertile land and very neat farms, no equipment or a boards lying around. Most of the barns are of this variety instead of the California style.

   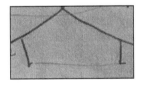

Nebraska style barns   **California style barn**

Well, have to take off. Let you know when I am in Boise.

Jack

130

Chapter 8

Gowan Field Boise, Idaho

212th Combat Crew Training School

78 – June 12th, 1943
Gowen Field officer's Club
Boise, Idaho
 Dear Mother and Dad,

It's 7:00 AM Monday morning and I just found out I don't have to report to our training classes until tomorrow. I arrive Friday night and they gave us the night to look over the town of Boise. Saturday morning we filled out a million papers and in the afternoon we had a physical which I passed okay. Sunday we didn't do much. Oh yes Saturday we were assigned to our crews and moved in with them. I like them very much so far; our pilot comes from Maine, our co-pilot from North Carolina, and our bombardier from Pennsylvania. I haven't met the enlisted crew yet. We live in a barracks like this.

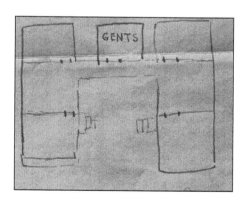

Diagram of Barracks Gowan Field Utah

 Six crews to each barracks, four men to each room. We have a negro enlisted man who cleans up the Barracks, makes our beds and shines our shoes (for 10¢) Back to Sunday, we didn't do much but I was issued some flying clothes such as a parachute harness, oxygen mask, goggles, helmet and a big thick coat and pants. It gets very cold at high altitudes and the B24 is pretty drafty I hear. I'm going to get my navigation equipment this morning. I took a look at our schedule for this second phase training and they keep us pretty busy all day. We will fly three days and the other three we spend in trainers where we practice navigation, or Bombing, or learn about guns and all the things we have to know. We are supposed to have Sundays off.

I am told we have one long flight to San Francisco and back later on. Woodland is directly in our path so maybe I'll fly directly over our house. Boise is a swell little town of about 30,000. It's kind of set in a valley right up against some mountains. Gowen Field is the best field I've ever been stationed at, the food and service is tops; tablecloths, dishes and even waitresses that serve you. The officers club is the best in the 2nd Air Force. They have everything from slot machines to classical records. They also stage dances here every Saturday night.

Well, this is about all I know as yet. Did you get my telegram and was it clear? I wanted the green flight jacket, that brown hat and the small radio if you could spare it. Jane must have brought mine home when going to New York and I thought just for eight weeks you could let me have the small one.

Well I'll have to get going.

Jack

79 – June 18th, 1944
Gowen Field
Boise, Idaho
Dear Mother and Dad,

Just phoned you, so there isn't much news. We work hard but they treat us goods we don't mind. We fly every other day and we have classwork on the others. We have to learn a lot about the ship and about each other's job. I am learning how to drop the bombs now.

Here is a typical day of flying. Up at 3:30 shower and eat breakfast. Report to the briefing room at 4:30 where we discuss the mission and instructions. We then put on our heavy flying clothes and report to the ship. We check everything on the ship and then load the bombs. We take off and go through the work. We each practice at operating the turrets and machine guns. We go bomb and practice formation flying and then land. This usually lasts about 5 hours.

Well, I can't think of anything more so I'll close.

Jack

80 – June 26th , 1944
H.B. C. Gowen Field
Boise, Idaho
Dear Mother and Dad,

Well, another interesting week has passed and another one coming up.

Our crew is beginning to click and we are learning something new each day.

Last Saturday we had an assimilated bombing mission in which six B 24's took off and bombed Wendover field Utah and Salt

Jack's War – Letters to home from an American WWII Navigator

Lake City and then returned to Boise. I was the lead navigator and even if it was just in the U.S., beads of perspiration stood out when they told me it was my responsibility to get them there. I almost did get lost at Wendover but came in all right. As we went over Wendover about 10 P47' rose and made passes at us. Our gunners had cameras in their guns to record their firing. I'm wondering if Bob wasn't piloting one of those P47's. That would be a unique way to meet him. Flew over the Great Salt Lake and got back just at sunset.

Received the camera and the film and the pictures thank you. I will send you a picture of my crew as soon as developed. We start flying every day from here on in so I have to get to bed.

Jack

81 – July 3rd, 1944
H.B. C. Gowen Field
Boise, Idaho
Dear Mother and Dad,

Pay day today so I better get rid of it before I spend it. A 2nd Lt sure can get rid of his money fast. Went down to Las Vegas and back last night. Well, have to report for flying. I guess you better invest this in the 5th War Bond or anyway you see fit.

Jack

82 – July 2nd, 1944
H.B. C. Gowen Field
Boise, Idaho
Dear Mother and Dad,

Just finished another week of training and really did accomplish a lot. The best part of it was today when I was headed

134

for lunch when I heard a familiar whistle and there stood Bob. Boy, was I glad to see him! He flew up from Wendover with three other fellows. We had lunch together then I had to report to the briefing room. He went down with me and got a good idea of what our job was like for they really had a mission planned out for us.

We were bombing Pendleton, Walla Walla, Spokane and Klamath Lake, but at the last minute our plane was jerked out for repairs so Bob and I just sat around and talked until he had to go. He sure flies a neat ship; P47 Thunderbolt.

What a week: Monday we had ten hours of ground school. Tuesday up at 3:30 and flying all morning. Wednesday the same thing. Thursday night we flew down to Las Vegas which is a celestial mission. Friday night we practiced bombing all night and likewise Saturday night. Boy we were really tired Sunday and it was a break we didn't have to fly. I just tried to phone you but you weren't in. (Probably over at the Eddy's discussing politics eh what.)

When are Jane and Claude due back and where are they going to stay? Is he still in his same outfit or is he being transferred?

Never did get to go on that trip in the mountains for we flew that day. Just got a letter from Hollis and he is down at Roswell N.M. in B 17 school.

I guess mother and Mrs Eddy are getting ready to throw F.D.R. out of office and escort Tom Dewey right up to the White House. I wonder if they will give a party this election night. Confidentially I think Earl Warren was the smartest man at the convention although Hoover made a good speech.

Well it's past 12:00 so-----

Jack

83 – July 14th, 1944
H.B. C. Gowen Field

Jack's War – Letters to home from an American WWII Navigator

Boise, Idaho

Dear Mother and Dad,

Well I guess I'm 21 today but I sure don't feel a day older than the day I graduated from high school. I could do the same things now as I could then except navigate and anybody with common sense could do that.

I read your financial report and it was very complete and really gives me a good idea of what I have. I didn't have the slightest idea up to now. I will be glad to take over the paying of my insurance premium and also you can change any names you want to on them for I have just given you Power of Attorney (Dad) which becomes effective today. I will send you a notice if they give me one. I also asked for a will but haven't the slightest idea of what it says or what I could will anybody.

The reason I haven't written sooner is that I have been flying and going to school day and night. When we do get a day off, we just hit the sack and sleep or go into town and have a wild time; they're both very restful from our schedule.

We have had quite a few trips that have been real fun. We have simulated bombing attacks going out in formation and putting cameras on our bombing sights. We went to Elko, Twin Falls and Burley and then home in the afternoon, and last Sunday we had a real long one bombing Ellenberg, Spokane, The Dalles, Pendleton, Baker and home. Boy, we sure saw some neat country and flew right by Mt. Hood and all along the Columbia River.

Last week they started processing us in preparation to leaving and that took all morning. In the afternoon I spent five hours in the Celestial "Nav trainer" and that night we were assigned to a Celestial mission to Sacramento. Well I tried to get a telegram to you to let you know I was coming. We were going to turn on the landing lights and search light and drop a smoke bomb for good measure but dam it I got lost due to a compass which was sixteen degrees off. I think we ended up over Stockton but still not sure. May get to come down again though. Be looking for me at night. I have told you before but here goes, I have received everything you have sent and thank you for all and also thank Mrs Leirers for her share in the cookies and keep them rolling. I like brownies or the ones with chocolate in them. Thanks for the birthday present. We don't leave for quite a while yet, around the end of July I think. I doubt if we get a leave, but maybe I will be lucky. You never can tell. Just got a letter from Linn Wilson. You can read it. Well that's all I can think of just now. The Democrat has stopped coming which make me mad because that is my only way of hearing about the town.

Jack

Letter from Linn Wilson:

June 22 1944
V-MAIL

> *Lt Linn Wilson 0717714*
> *APO 16209-CJ-94*
> *9PM., N.Y, N.Y.*
> *Dear John,*

Hi Fella, how's the "man from Texas" doing these days? Navigating as usual? Better do a lot of it as it will come in might handy over here, believe me.

Been wondering where you are - heard you were in Sioux City – wish I could have seen you- perhaps it won't be long. We arrived in Northern Ireland after quite a trip over- saw quite a few places – then to England "somewhere" – you know how it is – "no speka da English".

Jack's War – Letters to home from an American WWII Navigator

Hugh and I have at last been separated though I expect to see him shortly. He and Elsie were together for quite a while before he left. They are really a pair together believe me. Write when you get a chance. Tell your folks hello for me. My mother sends her regards to you, also.

Your buddy, Linn

A letter to Jack's Father from Jack's mother on the occasion of Jack's 21st birthday:

Friday July 14th, 1944
San Luis Obispo
Gracie's apt. (Beth's sister)

Dearie:-

Twenty one years ago! Do I remember correctly, that I went with you to work? and about noon presented you with a son. The years have passed quickly, in retrospect too quickly! But that son Jack is now a man and serving his country in a way to do us both great credit and you and I are very proud of him. I'm sorry we cannot be together today, but war changes everything. I shall think of you and Jack all day as we drive onto Riverside and meet our daughter Jane and her husband. The trip so far has been fine! Fog here this morning, not too warm at any place yesterday.

Much, much love,

Beth

84 – July 15th, 1944
H.B. C. Gowen Field
Boise, Idaho
　　　Dear Mother and Dad,

Just sending you these two important papers (will and power of attorney) because I guess you two are the ones who need

138

them. Also had some pictures taken but they turned out lousy so I guess you can burn the lot of them if you like.

Received the papers from the county clerk and will try to get them filled out.

I didn't have any allotment made out to send to you each month for I would rather have the money in case I wanted to buy something or incurred any debts. Well we're flying at night so

Jack

July 25th, 1944 Note from jack's father:

Jack surprised us this P.M. Arrived from Boise- came by auto with Sgt. Phillip Rose of Rt 2 Box 271 Chico California- will remain with us until July 30th when he leaves for Herington Kansas- "staging area"- he leaves by plane T.W.A. from San Francisco.

Crew 5750 Gowan Field Boise Idaho July 23, 1944

Crew
Porter Whittier   2nd Lt- Pilot- Maine
James King   2nd Lt -Co-Pilot – Greensborough, N.C.

Leo Garrigan   2nd Lt -Bombardier- Penn
Jack Woolsey   2nd Lt -Navigator - Woodland Ca
Auburn Phelps   Corp.-Engineer - Wisc
Don Jennings   Corp. -A. Gunner -Calif.
Anthony Lorraine   Corp.-Radio Operator-
Charles Landrum   Corp.- Asst. Engineer/Top Gunner-Oklahoma

Raymond Van Liew   Corp. -Nose gunner- Kansas
Chester Burger   Sgt.-Tail Gunner – New Jersey

Jack's Plane Boise Idaho 1944

The officers of Bomber Crew 5750 Whit, Jack, Les, King

Lt. Whittier Pilot

Lt. King Co-Pilot

Lt. Woolsey Navigator

Lt. Garrigan Bombardier

Chas. Rhode Navigator 5739 Montana

Jack "getting a fix"

Jack King and Whittier

Corp Van Lieu Nose gunner

Sgt Burger Tail Gunner

Corp. Landrum Asst. Engineer and Top Gunner

Corp. Phelps Engineer

Corp Jennings A gunner

Corp Lorraine Radio man

Sgt Burger at work

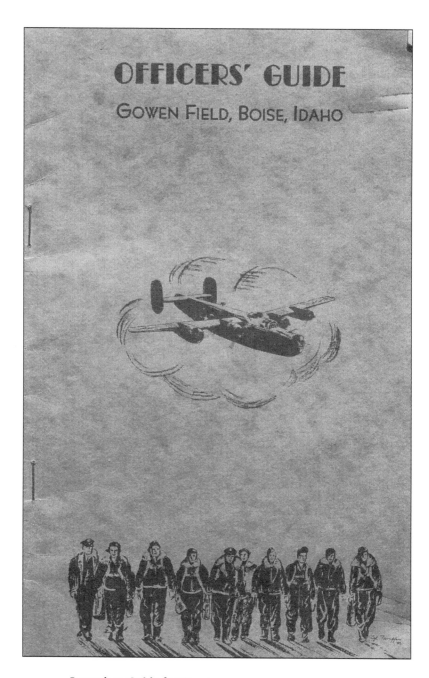

Procedure Guide for Gowan

Jack's War – Letters to home from an American WWII Navigator

Chapter 9

Going to War

85 – August 2nd, 1944
℅ General Delivery
H.A.A. F.
Herington Kansas
    Dear Mother and Dad,

Had a swell trip back, only way to travel. Almost lost my seat in Los Angeles. Tried to phone Jane but she was not home. Caught a cattle car (bus) out of Wichita and arrived in Herington at 12:00 A.M. or P.M. it is about the size of Winters only twice as hot and humid. I haven't stopped perspiring since I arrived and don't expect to stop until I leave.

There aren't any B 24s here so that means we go over on boats darn it.

We are all through our clothing process and also personal papers. Fixed up $150 allotment per month and I don't know where we are going but I guess it will be east. We are restricted to base tomorrow so will probably leave Friday.

Well, I'll right again there are new developments.

Jack

Personal Affairs Check Sheet

86 – August 3rd, 1944

Dear attorney,

You have the power and here are the orders. Would you please deposit them in my checking account at the Bank of America.

Jack

Jack's War – Letters to home from an American WWII Navigator

87 – September 3rd, 1944
   V-Mail
   APO 16399-BA-28
   ℅ P.M. NY.NY.
   Dear Mother and Dad,

It's been so long since the last letter I can't remember whether I wrote it at Herington or not. Well we left Herington by troop train and what a ride that was. We arrived on the east coast within twelve hours I ran into Bob. We had a swell time and spent one night in N.Y. We are now on the ocean in a convoy and to say the least conditions are crowded. Bob and I aren't on the same ship but hope to meet wherever we go. I hope you are all okay Toots and the horses too. Will give your regards to Ken.

   Jack

Chapter 10

The E.T.O.

88 – August 28th, 1944
 V-Mail
APO 16399-BA-28
℅ P.M. NY.NY.
     Dear Mother Jane and Dad

    I guess I can include Jane now, can't I. I am somewhere in England processing again, Bob and I are at the same place but he has left to go to school as I am doing tomorrow. We go to school for two weeks and then I guess we get to go to combat. I sometimes doubt if I'll ever see action. England, it's just like you see in pictures, very green with red brick houses. You can tell there is a war on over here because everything is rationed. That sure was too bad about Pete Watts. I think it's a good idea to bring Koli in this winter and of course Jane can work with him all she wants too but don't let all our friends on him and don't jerk his mouth too hard. I can't say all I'd like to due to the strict censorship. Don't forget to send me films (120) and also if you have any spare candy, gum or cookies. Everyone on the crew is well and raring to go. Will try to look up Roy Barnes. I think you ought to write air mail instead of V-Mail for it is much quicker. Just found out you can't cash checks in England so my checking account is of no value but will continue it anyway. What is Claude doing now? I hope he gets into something he likes. I like it here in England and everything is very good considering there is a war on.

    Jack

89 – September 3rd, 1944
 V-Mail
APO 16399-BA-28
℅ P.M. NY.NY.

Jack's War – Letters to home from an American WWII Navigator

Dear Mother, Jane and Dad

Well here I am in Ireland but as usual can't say where. We are over here preparing for combat but our training is also a secret but I can say it is very good. They don't fool around here like they so in the states and the instructors are all ex combat men and know their stuff. Ireland isn't bad at all. The country is very green and 80 acres is a huge ranch. You see plenty of the old time life but also the modern too. We went into Belfast last night and it is just like S.F. rationing isn't too bad here and we get very good food. The girls know all the American sayings and even know how to jitterbug. Bob and I are now together. Well going to bed.

Jack

90 – September 9th, 1944
V-Mail
APO 16399-BA-28
℅ P.M. NY.NY.
Dear Mother, Jane and Dad,

Well how is everybody at home? I get Dad's V-mails but mothers and Jane's are rather few and far between. I'm still in Ireland and enjoying every minute of it. The training is tops and we have been having quite a time in Ireland namely Belfast. I guess you are all getting ready for Mike it must be quite exciting. Wish I could be there, but will celebrate over here anyway. We ought to be assigned to a Bombardment Group pretty soon and then "Watch out Adolf". I think General Eisenhower and I can wind this thing up in short order and then I'll confer with Mc Arthur about this Jap issue. Well write more often. Regards to Toots, Koli and Star

Jack

91 – September 10th, 1944
V-Mail
APO 16399-BA-28
℅ P.M. NY.NY.
Dear Dad,

Just received your letter dated August 27 so you can see the mail service is poor. In fact, it got me to thinking just how long it took your letter thirteen days and the distance it travelled and I figured your letter traveled twenty miles every hour so you can see that if you could line up a couple of fast horses you could get them over here just as fast. Well what I wanted to tell you that as Jane is going to have a baby and with me not being there, would you take some money out of my account and buy the baby a $50 war bond or deposit $50 in the baby's account. You get the idea don't you? Well everything is going okay with 5750 and everyone is ready to go. Ought to be in action in about a week.

Jack

92 – September 17th, 1944
389th Bomb Group 564th Sqd APO 558
℅ P.M. N.Y. N.Y.
Dear Mother Jane and Dad,

Sunday night here in England and I guess you are just finishing your lunch. Hope mother is okay and with you now. Sorry you haven't received any letters from me but I'll keep writing anyway. Don't get any letters myself except Dad's V-M. Oh yes I'm back in England and have been assigned to the 389th Bomb Group, which is one of the best over here. They were in that famous Ploesti Oil Field raid about a year ago. We have good quarters, food and equipment. We are going to school again but are just about ready to let the Jerrys have it. I personally think it will be two or three weeks before we go on our first mission though. We may get a chance to haul some supplies when it will do the most good. We are always

Jack's War – Letters to home from an American WWII Navigator

going to school and learning something new each day. We usually have a full day whether we fly or not. Heard from Bob and he is going to school too. How about sending me a couple of sheets if you have some extra ones. Running into a lot of friends of mine in England. The beer Isn't too bad over here, but there isn't too much to do, but I seem to be able to spend all my money. Half of my clothes are one in my foot locker which they say will never catch up with you till you're ready to come home. Well, have to hit the sack.

Jack

93 – September 4th, 1944
389th Bomb Group 564th Sqd APO 558
% P.M. N.Y. N.Y.
      Dear Dad,

Well still writing, but no letters for a week and a half so you see you are not the only one receiving mail.

Haven't flown lately and things are going so well that I sometimes doubt if we'll even get any combat time. We have been having lots of fun just seeing some of the sites close by. Celebrated this Groups 200th mission yesterday and had quite a few dignitaries present. You know the leading Generals in the 8th Air Force. Saw an elderly gentleman in a naval uniform and they told me later that he was the king of Yugoslavia but I'm not sure.

Say would you order me some flowers for Jane when she gets in the hospital. Thank you "attorney".

Say on what date did you sail over on the Leviathan? A buddy of mine Chuck Rohde's father, you have his picture, came

162

over on it too and we were wondering whether it was the same time. Well nothing new.

Jack

P.S. Send me some 120 films if possible.

94 – October 5th, 1944
389th Bomb Group 564th Sqd APO 558
℅ P.M. N.Y. N.Y.
Dear Mother Jane and Dad,

Just received some letters so I guess the mail service is picking up. Glad to hear mine are coming through now. I'll bet your all getting ready for Mike. How is it going feel being a Granddad and mother? Hope Toots doesn't feel too bad about it.

Things are going well over here, still haven't flown a mission yet but have been assigned a place and we ought to be ready any year now. Flew over Stratford Von Avon "Bill Shakespeare's home" the other day. You can cover half of England in one flight it's so small. Weather hasn't been too bad lately but when you fly there is usually about a 9/10 cloud coverage so the Navigator has to be on the ball and bring them right over their field but it isn't hard with a certain new navigation aid.

Our room is beginning to look like something, we have it full of maps and pictures. Jane's and Claude's is on the dresser, and I have colored pictures mounted right above my bed so all I have to do is turn my head to see mother out in the yard or Jane on Jo and Dad and myself out in the drive way.

We get a lot of fun out of listening to the German programs and propaganda. They have by far the best music at night, and I think they would all elect Dewey unanimously. They try to break up British and American unity and its really funny to listen to them rant

Jack's War – Letters to home from an American WWII Navigator

and rave. They do have quite a lot of popular music which surprised me.

I guess Claude is pretty mad about being stuck down in L.A. fighting fires, and I can sympathize with him; this laying around doing nothing is the worst thing in the world. I read in the Stars and Stripes they were going to get rid of some army jeeps and I wondered if he knew anything about it and if he could get a hold of one. I wish he would buy it and I would pay him for it through Dad.

What are your ideas about ranching after the war? Where would you want to ranch and how extensively would you want to start out? I think it would be a good idea, but I do think we ought to have somebody with a little experience to help us along, and I have a person in mind. Well just a thought for the day. Don't forget the films and thanks for sending the sheets and stuff I hope I get them pretty soon. Don't be giving any false information to Paula or Jay about what I'm doing. Regards to Toots an Koli and Star.

Hurrah for Dewey

Jack

95 – October 9th, 1944
389th Bomb Group 564th Sqd APO 558
℅ P.M. N.Y. N.Y.
Dear Jane, Mother and Dad

Well how are things coming at home these days? I imagine the house is a little on edge with the day so close.

Well we finally got in the fight the other day and what a day it was. We really got a good initiation. I think the Jerries knew we were up there for they really slammed home the flak and it was very accurate. When I saw these black puffs of smoke right out my window I just got right back to work and tried not to notice it. They shot up our hydraulic system and we had to land in one of the emergency fields in England. We have had another mission and it wasn't very tough. No kidding it might not sound like fun but so far I have enjoyed every minute of it and wouldn't trade places with anyone for all the money in the world. Well, no news lately. Say would you send me some golf balls. I have a chance to get on the field team. Also send me the pictures

Well regards to Toots and the horses.

Jack

P.S. For gosh sake I hope you don't name the baby Wendy Ann

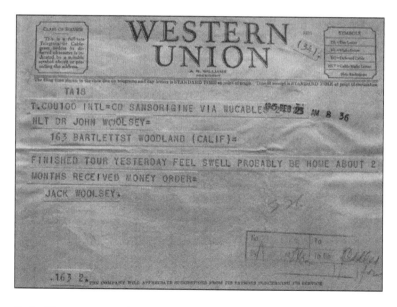

End of tour message home

Jack's War – Letters to home from an American WWII Navigator

96 – October 17th, 1944
389th Bomb Group 564th Sqd APO 558
% P.M. N.Y. N.Y.
　　　Dear Mother, Jane and Dad,

Well just got back from the Vaterland and had a swell trip. Went over a town (later noted to be Cologne) which is very much in the limelight right now but didn't stop to inquire how things were going. There goes the radio telling what we did today.

By the time this letter reaches you I will undoubtedly be an uncle. Congratulations all around. I hope Claude was there for the event and kept his shirt on.

Have been getting some letters from you over a month old. Have received four colored pictures and they are swell, have them mounted up on the wall already. Looking forward to the packages you sent but and it will probably be in the spring before I get them.

Had a forty eight hour pass last week, and we went down to London. It is just another large town robbing the American soldiers blind. Saw Buckingham Palace, Parliament buildings, 10 Downing St., West Minister Abbey, Big Ben, Thames Estuary. They didn't impress me very much but then England isn't a very impressing nation as far as sights to see.

London has taken a terrific pounding from the robot bombs but has stood up well under it. A couple have landed near our field but they don't bother me.

Jim King (co-pilot and myself were trying to find something to do the other day when we saw a "sign-up" for golfers. We looked into it and found they wanted some men to represent the field against the local country club. Well we signed up and went on our Sunday afternoon and with some Red Cross clubs and balls, King and I got matched up with a couple of middle aged Englishmen, a

166

Mr Jackson and Mr Dougall. King and I were a bit wild and they were typically English. Right down the middle of the fairway and very deadly with their irons. We played for holes (low ball) three points for the eighteen. They were swell fellows, and we had a lot of fun. They jumped into an early lead and had us two down at the end of the first nine but by that time I had my woods down and was blasting them 250 yards. Between the two of us we came to the 17th hole one down and I took the 17th with a par to even us up. On the 18th we had them pressing pretty hard and they both drove off into the rough with King and I straight down the middle. Well Jackson made a sensational shot out of the rough and approached to within fifteen feet of the pin lying three. Well as usual with my weak iron game, I was thirty feet away and lying three. Well I stepped up and tapped it and it headed right for the cup but when it got there and ran around the back door and hesitated but finally dropped. I thought we had the match won, but Jackson was a fighter and sunk a beautiful putt to tie the match up which was a good way to end it. We went in later and had sandwiches and tea and really met the better class of Englishmen who are all very nice and not at all deadpans. Mr Jackson invited us over to visit his school. He runs a large boys school here in town. The Red Cross has two very good sets of clubs and we plan to play as much as we can. All we need are some golf balls, so if you could lend us some it sure would appreciate it. I think in a can would be best.

Porter, Jim and I fly as much as we can for we all work together and like to fly. Yesterday they wanted us to test a ship, and so I planned a little cross country for us and we saw the Bristol Channel, Cardiff, North Hampton, Oxford and Birmingham. We took along a couple of Canadian seamen who wanted a ride and they promised to give us a ride in their P.T. boat if we got leave and came down to see them.

Say, I know you and Dad give a lot of money to the Red Cross and I'll tell you one thing they do. Every time we come down from a mission they have hot coffee and sandwiches ready for us.

It's not much, but it sure is good. We also get a shot of whiskey which "ain't bad".

Well got to go to dinner. Don't worry about me for I've never had such a good time in my life. King and I eat this combat up, and if we had our way we'd be out every day. Well as they say in jolly old England

Cheerio,

Jack

P.S. Regards to the niece or nephew and Claude. Received my ballot the other day and cast a vote for Dewey. Didn't understand some of the propositions but voted anyway. Dewey's speeches sound pretty good in comparison to Roosevelt's mudslinging. How anybody can swallow his line is more than I can see.

Bought a bike the other day and some clothes in London so only have a few schillings left but one doesn't spend too much here.

Well time to close.

Jack

Jack and his Bike

97 – October 26th, 1944
389th Bomb Group 564th Sqd APO 558
℅ P.M. N.Y. N.Y.
    Dear Jane, Mother Dad and niece,

    Just got back from the Reich and found the telegram waiting with the good news. That sure is swell and glad everything is going okay on the home front. How was Claude, was he very nervous? Weather is beginning to slow our operations up but we're still flying quite a bit, but not enough to suit me. As it stands right now I really enjoy combat more than anything I've ever done, but they say after a few missions you begin to sweat them out, but I don't think this will be the way for me, for it's too exciting.

    Have received all the colored pictures in fine shape and they are sure swell, have mounted them all mounted in my room and you ought to see the boys come in and crowd around them.

    Gee, I don't know what to get you all for Christmas. They practically have nothing to sell over here. Would you take care of

Jack's War – Letters to home from an American WWII Navigator

the relatives for me and I'll see what I can get over here. You can send me the bill or take it out of my savings.

Went to the dog races the other Saturday and had a grand time. We bet on the dogs and I won two pounds ten schillings (ten dollars) and two of our other friend lost all they had and are still trying to find the dog they bet on in the last race.

Received some candy from Paula in a tin can and it was in good shape so guess all yours will be okay when it arrives. Have another forty eight hour pass coming up this Sunday, but as yet don't know what I'll do. Would like to visit Bob but don't know where he is.

In the telegram there was a question "Are you ill?" Naturally I'm dying of pneumonia and arthritis. I know whose idea that was, and thought it was very subtle. When we don't get letters over here, when they mean so much, we chalk it up to the mail service or that there is nothing new at home and let it go at that. Well enough said (I hope).

Just read the bulletin board and we're up tomorrow so I guess I'll hit the sack. Regards to Toots and the horses. Gurgle at the baby a couple of times for me.

Jack

98 – November 2nd, 1944
389th Bomb Group 564th Sqd APO 558
℅ P.M. N.Y. N.Y.
   Dear Mother, Jane and Dad,

Well, have things quieted down at home or are you up at all hours of the night? Things are more or less always up in the air at bomber base and I'm getting used to it.

Flew a mission today and had a swell time. It was clear at the target and we could see our bombs hitting. Boy you can't imagine what a job they do until you see it. You see a nice little red house and then a blinding flash and no more house.

Had another forty eight hour pass this last weekend and went to London alone and had a marvelous time. Got in on the Red Cross tour of the high spots. We were shown around by a French woman who was a scream and knew all about the English and didn't spare any of the stories. Found out the story Behind Piccadilly Circus and how the saying "Cock and Bull Story" got started: There were two bars in London, one the Bull and the other the Cock. A story would start down around the bar at the Cock and then they'd go down to the Bull and enlarge upon it, thus the saying. The Cock is still operating just as it was in the old days, and we had a few drinks there. She took us to lunch at an exclusive French restaurant and it was the best meal I've had since leaving the States. I also went out to Madam Tussaud's wax museum which was extremely good. The pamphlet will give you an idea of what they have. One night I went to a play which was very funny. Had to come back after that, but looked around for some Christmas presents and honestly I just can't find a thing. I'll tell you what I'll do, I'll send you your presents when I find something I think you will like. I hope you will take care of the relatives for me.

Just received your packages. They arrived fine (two packages). You don't have to wax the tops though for that paraffin just cracks and breaks off. Received the films and thanks a lot of everything we sure do enjoy them. Thought you might be interested in the set up over here.

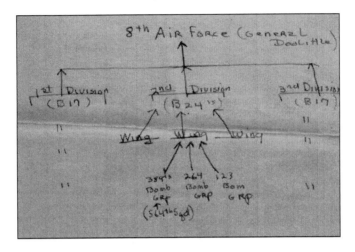

Schematic of the 8th Air Force

Well we're alerted for tomorrow so will knock off.

Jack

Any more films would be appreciated, also any more colored pictures.

99 – November 7th, 1944
389th Bomb Group 564th Sqd APO 558
℅ P.M. N.Y. N.Y.
    Dear Mother, Jane and Dad and Wendy Ann and Toots,

Well here I am again but not much news just about the same routine as I've been doing. Been flying quite a bit, but the weather is slowing us up and things will probably go pretty slow from here on. Still having the best time of my life and enjoying every minute of it.

I thought maybe you would like to know what a combat day consists of so here goes. We're logging time in the sack and all of a sudden a light goes on and an orderly says breakfast at 4:00, briefing at 5:00. We groan and moan and then jump in our clothes and peddle down to the mess hall and down our two eggs and then head down to the briefing room where we all gather. First "intelligence" gives us the target and details about it and the bomb run into the target. Then we get the weather for the trip (winds, temperature and clouds). After that the Command Pilot give us details about the formation code-words etc. After this we break up into separate briefings; Pilots, Bombardiers, Navigators. Over in the Navigator's room we draw our courses on our maps and make out our flight plans. Then we go to our lockers and put on all our clothing, heated flying suits, gloves, boots, May Wests→ (life preservers) etc. then we get into trucks and are taken out to the planes. We are always a little early and have time for a cigarette and plenty of jokes about the flak or "tour of the Ruhr" with the 389th. Then we taxi out and take off and form over the field and line out for the target. Then we just fly the mission and come back. After the landing, trucks take us back and we are interrogated by Intelligence and have a shot of whiskey plus some sandwiches and coffee. After we get through we peddle back to the barrack in hope of a letter and then back in the sack. Boy you would be surprised how fatigued you can get working under combat conditions. I'm busy practically every minute in the air, but this is what I like, so you can see why I'm so much happier over here than in the States. Well if weather permits I think we will pay the der fuhrer a call tomorrow.

Jack

100 – November 8th, 1944
389th Bomb Group 564th Sqd APO 558
℅ P.M. N.Y. N.Y.
    Dear Dad,

    Well thought I'd better check up with my attorney as to how my financial status was. I've looked into my allotment of $150

Jack's War – Letters to home from an American WWII Navigator

that is supposed to deposit in the bank each month. It started August so there should be $150 of August, $150 of September and etc. for October. Now when the bank get the money there should be some kind of notice out as to what month it was taken out of. If you will find out what month the $150 was taken out for and send me some kind of official notice, I can get the money refunded here for August and September. I also bought a $50 war bond when in Ireland and it should be sent to you or mother. If you haven't received it let me know.

We are enjoying the Christmas tins, thank a lot. As for the Democrat, I haven't received one copy.

Say if you ever get a chance to get a hold of some fur lined or wool lined gloves I sure could use them. Also if you would like to send some more food, we would like that too. We like the Velveeta cheese with some soda crackers especially.

Well, that about all for now.

Jack

101 – November 19th, 1944
389th Bomb Group 564th Sqd APO 558
HPO 558 % P.M. N.Y. N.Y.
     Dear Mother, Jane and Dad,

No news from the ETO due to the foul weather we're having over here, but just wanted to thank you for the Christmas packages which are coming in everyday now. Got 2 from Jane yesterday and two from Mother today. Boy! Are we loaded. Jim's getting his and so are all the boys in the barracks. Received the sheets and the films inside the candy thanks a lot.

Haven't done anything but sweat out the weather and sleep till 12:00. Just got done doing my laundry, so I'm set for four more weeks. Well thanks again for all the candy.

Jack

P.S. If you get a chance send my harmonica over.

102 – November 16th, 1944
389th Bomb Group 564th Sqd APO 558
HPO 558% P.M. N.Y. N.Y.
Dear Mother, Jane and Dad and Wendy Ann,

Well not much news from here, been idle for a week due to a two day pass and bad weather. Stayed right on the base due to lack of funds and sleep but had a good time anyway sleeping till twelve in the morning. On one of the afternoon we checked out a B24, just the three of us Whit, King and myself. I doubled as engineer and we went up and they practiced landings and then we went up to about 6000 feet and they let me take over. Really had a lot of fun and can handle it pretty good now. When we came down they let me land it, of course Whit was there correcting me, but it wasn't a bad one.

Just received the sheets you sent, thanks a lot. I think they will help a lot. Well there isn't much else to tell. Send me Bob's and Hollis's addresses for I've lost track of them.

Here's a diagram of my room. First to answer a few questions; I have my footlocker with me and listen to my radio every night. I can't tell you the number of missions I have to complete to get home. But the way I feel now I wouldn't quit for a million dollars.

Well this is where we live:

Jack's War – Letters to home from an American WWII Navigator

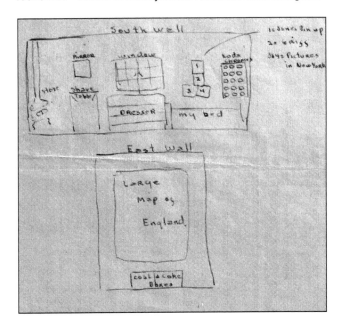

Jack's Room

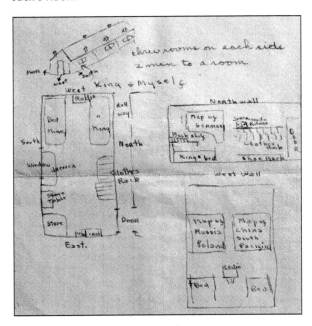

The Layout of buildings

Our room was practically bare when we started but we have built and painted in our time off and it's really pretty good now. Of course all the bare spots on the wall are rapidly being covered by pin-up pictures which are extremely easy on the eyes. Had an hour of snow the other day but it all melted right away. You ought to see me in my "long johns".

Jack

103 – December 3rd, 1944
389th Bomb Group 564th Sqd APO 558
HPO 558 ℅ P.M. N.Y. N.Y.
Dear Mother, Jane (Wendy Ann) and Dad,

Just received your letter of Nov. 6th so you can see we'll just have to grin and bear it. I think the V-Mail is faster but I can't read half of them and I always look forward to a colored picture in your other letters. I'm sorry I haven't written in so long but I have been rather restless of late due to the weather and other things keeping us on the ground. Combat mission have become a passion with me and unless I'm flying I can't write. I have received more of your packages with the candy and films. Thanks a lot for everything we sure appreciate it. The toll house cookies and nuts were delicious. I have received food in packages from the Doughertys, Mrs. Day (Ike's mother), Cousin Helen, Aunt Grace and a swell pair of slipper from Uncle Leon. I'm sorry I'm not sending anything for Christmas this year but England doesn't have much to offer, and things are pretty high anyway. Please explain this to the relatives.

We haven't been doing much due to the weather but let me tell you the German Luftwaffe is not dead by a long shot and the missions are getting pretty rough, but don't you ever worry about me. They couldn't touch us with a ten foot pole. We've flown right through some thick flak but they just don't have our number.

Jack's War – Letters to home from an American WWII Navigator

Anyway I enjoy every minute of it and wouldn't trade places with anyone in the world.

Yes, I do remember our old Maid and it sure is nice to be able to run in any night a see her and talk over old times. My letter finally caught up to Bob and he answered and he sure must be having a good time over there. That sure was good about him dropping supplies to the whole troops. I can't say too much but we work hand in hand with the infantry in Germany. We had quite a lot to do with the recent pushes our troops are making especially Patton's.

Well that's about all the news. I sure am sorry about Claude being shipped to Arkansas and especially into the infantry when he has trained for several other things. Dad, you just don't know how it is to be ordered to run like hell, so you stand in line for several months until they decide what to do with you, and things don't usually turn out for the best or become adjusted. Take myself, I could have been over here six months ago if I hadn't been delayed at every place I was and you just don't run up to your C.O. and tell him your troubles, for most of the guys don't give a dam about you and worry only about getting ahead themselves. I'm not trying to give you all lecture or cry about my troubles for I Love it over here, but this idea that things always turn out for the best well I just can't see it. I'm glad to hear that Jane and Wendy Ann are doing fine but gosh that name; how will she feel when she's about sixteen year old and people call her Wendy Ann, well I don't mind if you don't. Just sending you some pictures I thought you might enjoy.

Merry Christmas to you all.

Jack

My new Battle jacket a Bristol flying boots

You can see Whit's first cigar had a profound effect on him

The crew

Three "Sad Sacks"

104 – December 14th, 1944
389th Bomb Group 564th Sqd APO 558
HPO 558 % P.M. N.Y. N.Y.
    Dear Mother, Jane and Dad,

    Just back from a two day pass. Spent one night in town and the other at Great Yarmouth. Didn't do much but it is good to get off the base once in a while. Great Yarmouth is a sea coast town but really nothing exceptional there. Haven't been doing much flying lately due to the weather, but we get one in every now and then. The other morning we were awakened and told to get out to a certain plane on the double to fly some brass down to London. This happens every now and then and we thought it was probably some colonel, so we took some time about getting there. Well when we pull up in the jeep by the plane there stands a colonel and beside him Major General "Ike" Kepner, Commander of the 2nd Bomb Division. Well he didn't say a word and neither did we. So we piled in the B24 and took him down to London. On the way down the General had to relieve his bladder so he grabbed the relief tube and proceeded to do so. It was rather cold about 5° below zero and the

Jack's War – Letters to home from an American WWII Navigator

thing froze up on him causing him quite some embarrassment when it overflowed on his pants. He mumbled something about the dam ship not being taken care of and kept very quiet the rest of the trip. Actually he is a very capable General and very highly thought of over here. After we landed he complimented Whit on his flying and thought the trip was very good on the whole.

Well not much news. Got a few "October" Democrats the other day and noticed the high school football team wasn't doing too well. Haven't heard from any of you for a while but know you're okay.

Jack

105 – December 23rd, 1944
389th Bomb Group 564th Sqd APO 558
HPO 558 % P.M. N.Y. N.Y.
Dear Mother, Jane and Dad,

Just got back to the base after being away unexpectedly for a couple of days. In the meantime all your mail caught up with me. Two from Dad, three from Mother, one from Jane and a few others. Boy! Was I glad to hear from you. Got a tin of cookies from the Gay's

Well the weather had been bad and we had been trying to get in a mission for three days even going as far as Belgium before turning back on one of the days. Well, when Germany started "retreating" through our lines into Belgium we had to go weather or not. When we took off and we couldn't see ten yards in front of us, but Whit and King did a good job and we made it right down the middle of the runway and broke through the clouds at 3000 feet. We formed and went over and bombed our target and started back but when we went over the Channel we got word it was impossible to land at our base due to weather and we had to go to one that was clear. We made it all right but had to stay there for four days before we could get back, and if you can see what happens to us you can see what happens to the 8th A.F. then wonder if the Germans timed this counter offensive with the weather.

Of course it's very disappointing to have this happen, but I'm sure it will do us some good. Too many people here want to pack up and go home thinking the war was won, but I think we'll have to fight for every inch and I doubt the Germans will collapse.

From your letters I gather Thanksgiving was very successful even to grandpa wanting to know why I was dropping bombs on Germany. I hope Christmas will be a very happy one for all of you, and wish that I could be there, but honestly I am very happy with my work and doing a lot more good than just sitting around in the States like last year.

We hope to get a mission to Christmas Day and if we do we're going to take some chalk out to the planes and address the Christmas presents accordingly. Wish I could send you some sort of cablegram but they won't let us send any kind of word, so that is that. By the way I stopped that $150 allotment for 2 reasons. 1) I find I'm always running short at the end of the month and 2) No one in the finance department knows whether the money has been sent to the bank or not and or where in the heck it is, and you can't cash checks over here. If I get the money I know where it is, and I can send it home and you can deposit it for me and there will be no trouble.

Glad to hear Wendy Ann is coming along so nicely and thanks for the pictures of her. She will go to the head of my pin-up list. That's a good idea about bringing the horses in and you and Jane can train Koli as you see fit but always work for a tender mouth, most important I think. Well write again soon, boy, I sure like to hear from you.

Jack's War – Letters to home from an American WWII Navigator

Jack

106 – December 27th, 1944
389th Bomb Group 564th Sqd APO 558
HPO 558 % P.M. N.Y. N.Y.
Dear Mother, Jane and Dad,

Just to let you know that I was okay on Christmas and for that matter two days after. Sorry I couldn't send a cable but there was a restriction for ten days and you can see why. I spent Christmas day and day before delivering presents over the "Reich" and we really had a field day, boy we really went after them and blew everything up. We did miss turkey dinner on Christmas but as you know I like to fly so I didn't mind.

You want to know what "d" meant in the English monetary system. Well here goes:

£ (Pound) =$4

(Crown) =$1

(Florin) =40¢

("Bob") or schilling =20¢

(Sixpence) =1¢

(Pence) =2¢

(Guinea)= $1.20

We haven't named the plane and I doubt we will. We thought of a hundred names, but couldn't decide on any and now we think it would be bad luck to name it after coming this far. By the way I have 18 missions in now and that is just about half as many as I need.

Well, not much news so will knock off for now.

Jack

107 – January 9th, 1945
389th Bomb Group 564th Sqd APO 558
HPO 558 % P.M. N.Y. N.Y.
Dear Mother, Jane and Dad,

Just a note to let you know I've received most of your letters and packages and want to thank you for everything. The candy and the salted almonds were delicious and the golf balls with them. I haven't played since the last time, but I will use them or give them to the Red Cross so other soldiers can use them. The cans you send them in are very useful around the barracks and oh yes the money order was very appreciated and also the harmonica. I received all the Democrats boy what a load of them all the way from October up. Also received Dad's financial statement which was very good except that the money received Aug 7 was not the allotment money as that only goes to the bank so please check the bank and send me a signed statement saying that the $150 was not received so I can get it refunded here. Okay?

Yes we use the English money over here and you can catch on very fast. The English children aren't better educated that we are, far from it. They all stop school at fourteen and sixteen years and very few go on. Individually most Englishmen are pretty darn good Joes but as a whole you sometimes wonder how the heck they ever got their position and keep it with their policies, but I guess they know what they're doing. Have twenty four missions in now and ought to finish up in a couple of months. Had a close one the other day when a piece of flak came up through the nose but it didn't touch us.

Well that's all for tonight. Please don't send anymore cablegrams asking if I am Ill. It ceases to be funny. Oh yes please thank the Mc Narys, Griffiths and Russel Lowes for their Christmas cards.

Jack

108 – January 21st, 1945
13 564th Sqd APO 558
HPO 558 ℅ P.M. N.Y. N.Y.
389th Bomb Group

Letterhead form Jack's R&R

Dear Mother, Jane and Dad,

Well how do you like this, I've got a week's vacation right in the middle of a war zone and what a vacation it is. They call it the "flak house" but don't get any ideas for I'm not the least bit "Flaky" and there is absolutely nothing wrong with me. Everybody gets it as they approach the end of their tour and we had been flying like mad ever since the before Christmas so they just up and gave it to us and we up and took it, and here we are. The place use to be a big English Mansion which the Air Force took over and turned into a Rest Home for the officers of the combat crews. It is located in Southern England just about twenty five miles above (North) Bournemouth which is on the South Coast. The country is very beautiful with hills and trees and a few lakes and to top it off it snowed yesterday which makes it all the prettier.

The house is run by a Major in the A.C. and he has four Red Cross girls helping him and they do everything for you to make your stay as pleasant as possible. We sleep on real beds with clean sheets and you can sleep all day if you wish. I usually get up around 12:00 and get down just in time for lunch. There are plenty of things to do; they have a couple of horses you can rent which I did yesterday afternoon and had a swell ride even if it was in an English saddle. You can play badminton, table tennis, pool and they have plenty of books to read and phonograph recordings to play. About 4 o'clock we have tea and sandwiches and at 7:00 the bar opens up till 7:30 when we have dinner (all the meals are delicious). After dinner there is plenty to do, sometimes they have a show or like last night we went over the Station Hospital and went to the nurse's dance and what a time we had. This was the first time we'd been out with American girls since leaving the States. You should have seen all the Captain and Colonel Doctors waltzing around. I'll bet Dad had a pretty good time in the last war.

Oh yes, I forgot to tell you in the morning about 10:00 a butler comes in the room and sets a glass of grapefruit juice beside your bed and then pulls back the blinds. I expect King George down any day to make me an Earl or Duke. Oh yes, all during the day we run around in civilian clothes and only put uniforms on for dinner. Well I've got to go to lunch so I guess I'll close.

Regards to Wendy Ann, Toots and the horses. Oh rumor has it that you're not letting Toots on my bed, I think that's her undisputed privilege.

Well hope to see you in three to four months.

Jack

I got all your clippings and they were very interesting, don't see why the Chamber of Commerce can't freeze all the single girls left in town. Ha!

Jack's War – Letters to home from an American WWII Navigator

109 – January 24th, 1945
From the Flak House V-Mail
    Dear Uncle Leon,

Here I am at the rest home (no I am not having a nervous breakdown). This is really a good deal...as close to being home as possible. I have been sent down to get away from it all, and I am. We all run around in civilian clothes and somebody better start knitting the American Red Cross some sweaters according to our figures. The pants are usually bright and baggy. It reminds me of our old school days.

The food is out of this "GI" world of ours-five meals a day including juice served in bed by the butler. Rather than having the food thrown at us, it is served for a change. The house is an old estate turned hotel turned flak farm. It is wonderful to have soft sheets and running water that you don't have to run to far for. There is a ball room that they have turned into a gym. There are fireplaces everywhere and for a change they are all operational. It is really nice to be in a clean and tidy atmosphere.

We play golf tennis badminton, skeet shooting and fishing. I think I'll take a crack at most of these sports. By the time I get done with most of these that the five Red Cross girls keep egging you to do, I will have to go back to the base to rest.

Well gotta go, you have to dress for dinner-the only army touch. Hope I have a letter from you when I get back to the base.

Jack

P.S. This is a type form letter, but gives you an idea what I'm doing.

110 – February 4th, 1945
389th Bomb Group 564th Sqd APO 558
HPO 558 % P.M. N.Y. N.Y.
Dear Mother, Jane and Dad,

Another Sunday in England and the typical English weather but don't imagine Califironia Is all sunshine this time of year. We've been back from the flak home for a week now and haven't done very much. Been on two combat missions and they are getting pretty rough but it doesn't bother Whittier and Crew. Hollis is located about fifteen miles below me and I went down to see him the other day, but he was off on a practice mission so I missed him. Whit and I took a plane today and went down and buzzed his field but couldn't land. I'll get down to see him pretty soon though.

Please thank the following people for their swell Christmas cards if you have time: Griffiths, Mc Narys, Russell Lowes, Dr. and Mrs. Leivers, Mrs. Theircof, and Grandpa's housekeeper. Thank you

I think some of your mail was lost on some of those ships but I did receive a big box of candy form you and thanks a million, we did enjoy it. Glad to hear Wendy is doing so well. Just heard from Bob and he is fine and doing a swell job. I don't think his group protects us bombers but he helps the ground troops and sees plenty of action. Well still enjoying every minute of combat and don't worry. Ought to finish up by March or the 1st of April.

Jack

111 – February 17th, 1945
389th Bomb Group 564th Sqd APO 558
HPO 558 % P.M. N.Y. N.Y.
Dear Mother, Jane and Dad,

Well it's been a long time since I took the old pen in hand for I just haven't felt like writing. You see about a week ago I came down with a terrific sore throat on top of my usual English cough and just at the peak of my sore throat, I started cutting a wisdom tooth and my jaw swelled up and I couldn't eat and on top of this I was trying to fly. Well due to the sulfa pills and some salt water I managed to shake them off and not get locked up in the hospital for two weeks. My jaw is coming around and ought to be okay in another week. I'm not complaining, just telling you why I didn't write.

Just got a bunch of letters from you all and it sure was good to hear from you. Got a swell letter from Mr. Sandrock telling me about Bob and Bill and all about Woodland. The next time you see him Dad say hello and ask him about the pheasant that got in his bed during pheasant season. Oh by the way I got that $150 allotment cleared up. You see you get from example ($150 for September arrives in the bank in the middle of October). So you must have received one more payment after the last letter. You see that $100 money order is to help me get home in case I need it.

Received all your clippings and jokes and sure did enjoy them. That fellow from the hospital with trench foot must have had some experiences worth telling. Sure did enjoy Joy's clipping of myself. What a lot of baloney they write in that paper about the soldiers especially about the medals they get.

Spent an evening with Hollis in town and we sure did have a good time just shooting the breeze about home and what we've been doing. His base isn't very far from mine, and I plan to go visit him in the near future. Oh yes Dad, I enjoyed the clipping "So Ends the Year" that you sent me.

Jack

Whit's Happy Warriors after their last mission Feb 14th 1945. Jack is 21 years old

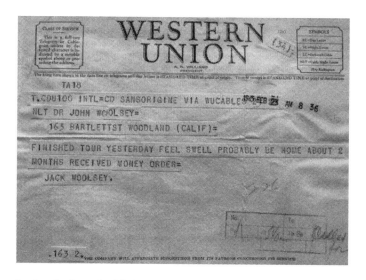

Last note from Jack's tour

Jack's War – Letters to home from an American WWII Navigator

Chapter 11

Finishing Up

Home From the E.T.O.

March 17th, 1945

Note from Jack's Father:

Jack arrived home march 17, 1945. Beth and I met him at Sacramento and then went to the house for breakfast. He and Jane then drove to Hamilton Field where he had to report. This evening we had a wonderful visit and he told us all about his missions and showed us his maps, air medals-Bastard Club membership.

Leave spent at two weddings and visiting and gaining 10 pounds.

April 9th, 1945

Leave over Left with Jane's car at 7:00 A.M. sharp with Mother. Stopped for breakfast to see Uncle Harold and Aunt Teresa and then onto Aunty Grace. Bid mother goodbye at Santa Barbara.

Jack's arrival home from war March 17 1945

112 – April 16th, 1945
SAAB R. S. #4
Santa Ana California
    Dear Mother, Jane, Wendy Ann and Dad,

    Well I can't say I enjoy the old army that much after that wonderful three weeks at home but the deal we're getting down here is about as good as we'll ever see. It takes about a week to get through the meetings and appointments that we have to make, and then we wait about a week more for our orders to come through, I have my last appointment tomorrow and that is with the classification officer. I'm pretty sure he will give me pilot training but you can never tell. If I do get it, I will probably be sent to one of the three Navigation schools in Texas where I will wait until my appointment comes through. They only allow so many officers into piloting a month and so they say the wait is from one to four months. They also tell me you're practically treated like a cadet again, but the way I look at it is it's worth any sacrifice I would have to make. I know some people will think I'm taking it so I won't have to go overseas again but honestly if I didn't have the opportunity to

Jack's War – Letters to home from an American WWII Navigator

do this I'd break my neck to go over to the South pacific for I really do like combat.

I passed the physical 100% and did so on all the exams they have given me so far. The rest of the time they have just been putting my records in shape and giving lectures on the home front.

The food down here is just about perfect and the entertainment, well you can see for yourself. I met up with a Capt. Williams who was in our group and he and I have been golfing everyday plus bowling (you'd better practice up Dad, but not on wedding nights), badminton, and tennis. Yesterday we visited Mr and Mrs Litchfield at Balboa and went sailing. They sure were nice to us and invited us back to sail their boat anytime (be sure and thanks Mrs Griffith).

I am getting Jane's car greased, oil changed, and lubricated and also if you find the car it would be possible, I would like to take it to Texas with me for they told us we get leave while awaiting our appointments to pilot training. Well. That's about all.

Jack

Goo goo ga blah boo blah wee dee da and drool

Uncle Jack

Arf Arf to you Toots

(Harold Schaffer just came in and we went bowling down at Balboa)

113 – April 23rd, 1945
SAAB R. S. #4
Santa Ana California
Dear Mother, Jane, Wendy Ann and Dad,

Well there really isn't much news to tell you after our phone call last night. I will remain down here until next Monday in hopes the car will show up. If it does show up I might be able to swing it so I can get a couple of days at home.

Yesterday Capt. Bob Williams (the fellow from the 389th), Harold Schaffer and I all went over to Santa Anita and saw Bob hope, Bing Crosby, Lt Ben Hogan, Olin Dutra, Betty Jameson and Bad (Didrikson) Zaharias play gold. It was really exceptionally good. This babe Zaharias can drive as far as the men and plays a wonderful game. Hope and Crosby are a scream besides being darn good golfers. Hogan was the best of the lot playing every shot to win. Hope keeps up a continual chatter with the crowd and he and Crosby also kid each other a lot.

I have seen Vern Wetzel who is in the hospital down here and also John Wetzel who is over at El Torro. Well that's all for now.

Jack

114 – May 1st, 1945
Postcard (On his way to Texas.)
 Dear Family,

 In El Centro Calif. Came by way of Pasadena. Spent night in Banning

 Plenty Hot, just drank 2 large Cokes and then 2 small ones. Going by way of Yuma Arizona

Jack

115 – May 2nd, 1945
Postcard
 Dear Family,

Jack's War – Letters to home from an American WWII Navigator

Spent last night in Tucson and eating breakfast in Benson right now. Boy is this country hot and desolate. Been living on cokes. Plan to stop at El Paso.

Jack

116 – May 3rd, 1945
Postcard
Dear Family,

162 miles out of Tucson Car broke down. Not even a rabbit in sight. Car being fixed. Having a wonderful time.

Jack

117 – May 4th, 1945
Postcard
Having cups of Coffee in Pecos Texas (Billy the kid country and he can have it) We're stuck in Roadforks New Mexico for 24hours and had a hilarious time. Will tell you about it in a letter.

Jack

118 – May 7th, 1945
SM AAF's Sqd 1
San Marcos, Texas
Dear Mother, Jane, Wendy Ann and Dad,

Well, this is my first day on the base and I've just been walking around checking in. As you might guess it is so sultry down here that you can't breathe without perspiring. I don't know my duties yet but I think we get a little school and a lot of P.T. and probably help out teaching the cadets. It isn't a bad base but I guess I had too much time at home to appreciate the best base in the Air Corps.

Our trip down was very successful and what a time we had. We drove down to Southern Calif. the first day and then crossed the

196

desert the next staying in Tucson. There were two other fellows from Sacramento with us. The next day was when our trouble started. We got 150 miles out of Tucson and we stripped the timing gear. Well I hitch-hiked into the nearest settlement (just across the New Mexico border) which was called Roadforks and that is just what it was, two roads that come together with a service station in the middle run by the unforgettable "Ben Clark" who pitched baseball in Texas for 30 years, raised 9 children, been married twice, worked for the Texas Rangers and now drinks a quart of whiskey a day to steady his nerves.

We phoned into Tucson for the timing gear and the dealer said he would put it on the next Greyhound coming this way which should arrive around 10 that night. Well the two boys couldn't wait so they took off via the thumb

So Harold and I had to wait. Well we went inside and began to get acquainted with Ben who showed us the family album between drinks and told us all about every home run he ever hit and how'd he'd turned the Yankees down. He then started to tell us about this crook he'd throw out the night before with a very vivid description in fact and before I know it he had reached down under the bar and was waving this six shooter and telling me how he had to conk him twice on the head to get him out. After this he had to show me all his guns and about this time another old timer strolls in a pulls out his six shooter and challenges Ben and myself to a contest. Well, I was a bit leery to go shooting because both men were pretty well oiled but I stayed well behind them and naturally they couldn't hit the broad side of a barn. Well that night we got so well acquainted with Ben that he went to bed and Harold and I ran the store and sold gas waiting for the part.

Well the part didn't show up by midnight so we decided to hitch hike to Tucson to see what was the matter. Well two cars pulled us driven by two ladies so we pointed the way to Tucson and asked them for a ride. The Mother said "Well I've heard so much about giving rides to soldiers" then she asked her daughter who said "sure given them a ride"". Well it turned out it was Mrs Bruton, (wife of General Bruton who was raised in Woodland and was brother of the late Judge Bruton).

Well we got to Tucson and got the part which hadn't been sent at all and hitch hikes back and put it bank on and bade farewell to Ben who had already drank his quart.

Well we drove all that night and had a 10:00 P.M. dinner in El Paso and kept going until we reached Dallas the next night and we just went to bed and slept. The next day Harold and I looked Dallas over and I hate to admit it but it is as good a town as there is in the U.S.

We went dancing that night and I left Sunday morning for San Marcos arriving at 5 in the afternoon.

This pilot training deal doesn't look too good but I'll stick around and see what turns up. Received Dad's letter and driver's license. Has Mrs Tracy phoned about the car yet? Here are some gas coupons for Jane's car. Cash them in even if you have to fill a drum with gas for I'm going to need it to get my car down here. Well, have to get going to supper.

Jack

Arf arf Toots

P.S. Don't worry too much about the gas coupons but fill up your car Jane.

VE DAY May 8th, 1945

Stars and Stripes Headline May 8th, 1945

119 – May 13th, 1945
SM AAF's OMS
San Marcos, Texas
Dear Mother, Jane, Wendy Ann and Dad,

    Well there is no news from Texas except it is so hot that you can't even sleep. The latest news is that they are going to stop pilot training altogether but nobody knows for sure. They are closing down San Antonio so we will probably go to Maxwell Field in

Jack's War – Letters to home from an American WWII Navigator

Alabama if we get in. They are starting to discharge the men on the field but officers have a different system than enlisted men, but I don't exactly want a discharge anyway. We are going to school to pass away the time, and tomorrow we are going to fly 8 hours to get our time in. We went up to Austin for the weekend and had a swell time swimming and horseback riding.

Well that's all the news for now. Don't forget to write once in a while.

Jack

120 – May 21st, 1945
SM AAF's OMS
San Marcos, Texas
Dear Mother, Jane, Wendy Ann and Dad,

Well another uneventful week has passed. We flew a couple of times and had a few classes but we are just killing time and you know how I hate laying around. We thought we were leaving this weekend but it fell through. We went up to Austin for the weekend and had a swell time on a picnic with some girls we know. We went swimming and had a picnic lunch. During the week we usually go into San Marcos at night to the show and bowl a few games. During the day we have classes and P.T. Well that's about all for now.

Jack

121 – May 30th, 1945
SM AAF's OMS
San Marcos, Texas
Dear Mother, Jane, Wendy Ann and Dad,

Just received your letter and the swell pictures. They sure are good. Sure am glad to hear Claude is safe and hope he gets home pronto.

I know my letters are poor but it is just a reflection of this base. They try to make us swallow a lot of this Boy Scouts stuff and consequently our moral is down to zero. We don't do much but we don't have much free time due to certain formations. About our only relaxation is to go swimming around 5 o'clock in town and our Saturday night and Sunday up in Austin. No I haven't contacted the Leakes yet and I am not taking any extracurricular stuff due to our indefinite status here. I have a pen but it leaks but I'll get another one. Hope you got my winter clothes all right.

Well I just can't think of anything more. Oh yes, I think President Truman is doing okay and war is okay. I am anxious to get out of this Boy Scout camp and into pilot training.

Jack

122 – June 4th, 1945
SM AAF's OMS
San Marcos, Texas
Dear Mother, Jane, Wendy Ann and Dad,

Just sent that telegram and know you are worrying about me. Well I'll give you the dope about the car. My friend and I (Richard L. Trice, from Virginia and was interned in Switzerland after his fourth mission) were figuring how much we were spending in Taxi cab fares the other day and we were so shocked at the result that we decided to buy a car. So we didn't want to spend much money so naturally we decided on a Model A Ford and we found a Sergeant who wanted to sell so we bought it and so far it runs like a top and is more fun than a barrel of monkeys. She looks something like this, tires are exceptionally good. Drove up to Austin in it and went on a picnic Sunday and had a lot of fun. Please don't worry about it for we are insured and it is just what we need to make this place enjoyable.

Jack and partner's Model A

The other day the big brass had a meeting and we combat Navigators were represented and from what I gathered they really had a session. Well the results were very satisfying for they are now treating us on an equal basis and have now cut out a lot of this nonsense they have been handing us. Boy I hope and pray that something will happen quick as I am growing stale in this Texas weather with no definite goal ahead of me.

I received the sheep material from Dr Hart and it looks very good. Please thank him for me a say hello to Dr Meade. The letters from Galen and Claude were very interesting and I sure hope Galen makes a complete recovery.

About the discharge, I wasn't up for one but I do have 77 points and they did discharge plenty of Navigators with 80 to 90 points, but what the heck. I don't want a discharge for a while anyway. Hope Uncle Leon is coming along fine and it clears up his stomach trouble.

Congratulations on your 56th birthday Dad and as Milan Weider once said….. Regards to all the animals and Mother keep up your good letters.

Jack

123 – June 11th, 1945
SM AAF's OMS
San Marcos, Texas
Dear Mother, Jane, Wendy Ann and Dad,

Well how's the home front holding out?

Right now I'm about the maddest man in the Air Corps. Sixty navigators were shipped to San Antonio last week and naturally my orders have been lost and naturally I did not ship out and naturally I'm so dam mad I could whip the japs single handed, but what hurts the most is that I heard they are getting ready to take another bunch of officers out to Lancaster Calif. for primary. Well they sent a tracer to Santa Ana to find out what happened so there isn't any doubt in my mind that I will be out of San Marcos by 1946 and out of Texas by 1950. My friend trice shipped out and left me the car so when I sell it I will give him half.

Went up to Austin again and called up Emma B. on the phone and plan to call on her sometime.

Received Uncle Leon's book and it looks pretty good. Glad to hear Kramer is getting a discharge. I rather expected him to stay on with aviation though. Harold Schaffer is sure getting a good deal. We flew over to Jackson Mississippi the other day and had dinner then came back that night. They keep us busy but it is just to kill time and we're not learning very much.

Sure would like to see Wendy Ann now. I'll bet she's as cute as a bug's ear. Oh yes I received the money $175 thanks very much for sending it. I didn't know what you did with that gas I sent home but if you have any spare tickets I sure could use them. They've rationed cigarettes to us (six packs a week) so that kind of put us behind the eight ball. Glad Claude is enjoying his work but sure hope he gets to come home. I remain (in Texas as usual),

Jack

Jack's War – Letters to home from an American WWII Navigator

124 – June 18th[th], 1945
SM AAF's OMS
San Marcos, Texas
Dear Mother, Jane, Wendy Ann and Dad,

Well another week has passed and nothing new just the same old routine. Sorry I didn't talk to you Sunday and wish you a happy father's day but I waited by a telephone and then gave up.

I'm glad that you paid my income tax for me. I guess I forgot to tell you I had it all made out at Santa Ana and put a note in my first payment asking them to acknowledge my first payment and forward instructions as to when they want the rest of the payments to my home address. They really are the most indefinite bunch I have ever seen. They don't seem to give a darn whether you pay or not and they don't hand out any receipts if you do.

Oh yes I answered Col Christophel's letter and long time ago so I'm squared out okay and will visit them when I go to San Antonio.

I just ran into a friend of mine who was in the same group as I was overseas and just got back. It seems as though they really had it rough after we left for 3 of those men who have their signature on my lucky Bastard card were killed in action. They lost three planes in one crack when a German jet shot down one, rammed another which caused it to crash into another. Sorry to hear about Galen. I didn't know it was so serious. I've been reading "Brave Men" by Ernie Pyle and quite a lot of magazines. The more I read about the German concentration camps, the more I wonder what they're stalling around with Goering and those other big named Nazi.

204

I met a fellow on this base by the name of Mc Cory Haines who was raised around Woodland and knows quite a few people. He just got his discharge and said if he was going through Woodland he would look you up.

Well I sure hope something happens this week for this place is really getting on my nerves.

Jack

125 – June 27th, 1945
SM AAF's OMS
San Marcos, Texas
Dear Mother, Jane, Wendy Ann and Dad,

Well it's still the same old story. Received a letter from the War Dept. asking for my waiver on a second tour of combat if they gave me Pilot Training. It consists of signing your name to a dotted line and should have been done at Santa Ana. It has cost me about 2 months of wasted time doing nothing. When I do ship out of here I think we will so to Maxwell Field Alabama to take our tests. This means I will get out of Texas, but I'll still be south of the Mason Dixon line.

I signed up for a $50 bond when they started the 7th W.L.D. so you'll get one each month until I stop the allotment.

I suspect Bob is home or at least in the States. Got a letter from Hollis and will be home sometime in July.

Perspiring yours,

Jack

P.S. Thanks for the swell letter Jane. I wrote Claude a letter last week.

126 – July 2nd, 1945
SM AAF's OMS
San Marcos, Texas
Dear Mother, Jane, Wendy Ann and Dad,

Nothing new down here. Still just waiting around. Received your package Dad. I cashed two checks before I got your book though one was $25 the other for $15 so I'll fix up my balance in this book. Well there isn't a darn thing to talk about so I'll just close.

Jack

P.S. Received both your letters Mom and Dad and the clippings about the Sproul marriages and also Dr. Ridenbachs letter. Oh yes I heard of that Marine indoctrination clipping. I really got a kick out of it. Do you want it back I'd like to keep it to show to the fellows in class. Here is picture of my latest jet propelled Ford, also enclosed are 2 $50 money orders.

Jack's Model A

127 – July 9th, 1945
Postcard for New Orleans
    Dear Family

Spent two days in the great town of New Orleans. Having a wonderful time

Driving my 1930 Ford and only one blow-out so far from Austin to here.

Jack

128 – July 13th, 1945
Sqd P. (Pre-flight)
Maxwell Field, Alabama
Dear Mother Jane, Wendy Ann and Dad

Well finally arrived in the "Cradle of the Confederacy" namely Montgomery Alabama, Maxwell Field. Had quite a trip out here in my 1930 Ford. Another Lt. and I drove out via Houston, Beaumont Texas, Lake Charles Baton Rouge La, New Orleans La, Mobile Alabama and Montgomery. We had a swell trip with only two forced stops. Drove straight through to New Orleans and arrived in N.O. at 7:00 Saturday night. We spent Sunday and half of Monday and saw all the sights and ate shrimp and French food till I thought I'd burst. We ate at Ardnaud's, Antoines and Brussards and spent a lot of time in the French Quarter just looking around. I drove out and had a look at Tulane College and Loyola but they aren't much. Louisiana is surprisingly a very beautiful state as is Mississippi especially around the Gulf where they have some beautiful mansions. We spent the night in Mobile Alabama and then drove up to Montgomery Alabama. Alabama is also very pretty with rolling hills and lots of pine trees. You see plenty of "darkies" and they all seem to have a mule and a wagon. They all looked as if they must have been related to "Enas Africanus".

This post is really very beautiful, something like Hamilton Field. I really don't know too much as yet to my future but will write and let you know.

Jack

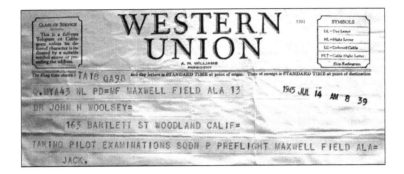

Confirmation Jack is taking the pilot examination

129 – July 20th, 1945
Sqd P. (Pre-flight)
Maxwell Field, Alabama
Dear Mother Jane, Wendy Ann and Dad

Still at Maxwell Field awaiting the results of our tests. In the meantime we are going to a stepped up pre-flight school which is rather a nuisance, but they tell us if we are classified pilots we have to pass tests in about eight different subjects before we can go to primary.

I haven't had any letter from you since I came here but I guess it takes quite a while.

This field is primarily a B29 training base. I went all though one the other day and they are quite some plane, but I think I prefer and lighter plastic ship.

Well that's all for now.

Jack

Note from Jack's father
July 23rd, 1945
Jack phoned from Maxwell Field and says "I'm a pilot now." His voice has its old enthusiastic ring.

Dad

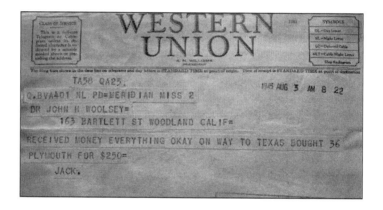

On the way to pilot training

130 – July 13th, 1945
Sqd P. (Pre-flight)
Maxwell Field, Alabama
　　Dear Mother Jane, Wendy Ann and Dad

　　Another Sunday has rolled around and I thought it was about time to answer some of you letters. Thanks very much for the swell presents; I couldn't ask for anything better. The payoff is that the fellow next door has a projector and a screen so I really had a night of it. You can imagine how long the candy and peanuts lasted.

Jack's War – Letters to home from an American WWII Navigator

That sure is swell that Hollis is home. I'll bet Bob will be in any day now. I received his letter and he was stuck at "Stone" in England for thirty days. Oh, yes, Linn Wilson is fine and has been transferred into A.T. C. with his permanent station at Love Field Dallas Texas so you can imagine how happy he is

Glad to hear you had a good time down at Menlo and that Mrs. Eddy is coming along so well. I hope you get up to Tahoe. I'd sure like to be with you.

There isn't much news from here. We go to about six hours of very uninteresting school each day and will probably have to take four more weeks of it. I heard a rumor that they were going to give some comprehensive exams sometime in the near future and if you passed you could be excused from classes. I will look into this. The weather is very humid down here with plenty of thunder showers.

Well there isn't much more to say. I didn't see the picture on Life so if you get a chance send it to me.

Jack

131 – July 31st, 1945
Sqd P. (Pre-flight)
Maxwell Field, Alabama
Dear Dad,

Well just got paid so I thought I'd better get rid of this before I lose it. Not much doing around here except school. I took some exams today but don't think I did too well.

The war is going good, I hope I get a chance to get through pilot training before it winds up. Well guess that's all for now.

Jack

P.S. Thanks a million for the Kodachromes. They really took me home for an hour. You know I'd like to have a nice little camera to take some pictures with. If you locate one you think worthwhile, I'd be glad to buy it.

132 – August 8th, 1945
Class 46-B Sqd 1
Goodfellow Field San Angelo Texas
Dear Mother, Jane, Wendy Ann and Dad,

Well I finally arrived in San Angelo early Monday morning in our 1936 Plymouth. We only had one blowout and didn't have a bit of trouble getting a new tire from the ration board in Jackson Mississippi. Spent one day in Austin Texas and then came here.

This place is really out in the desert but the town of San Angelo isn't bad, with a population of 45,000. We haven't done anything but check in and check out field but ought to start flying in a couple of days.

They have gone back to the prewar system of training and that means all your training fields are in Texas and fifteen weeks for each course (Primary, basic and advanced) so you can see I'll be a whole year in training. I hope this atomic bomb finishes up the war up in a couple of months though.

Got a swell letter from Claude. Will write you more later. Got the Kodachromes. They are swell.

Jack

V J Day
August 15th 1945

August 15th, 1945 Woodland Democrat

Chapter 12

The War is Over

133 – August 21st, 1945
Class 46-B Sqd 1
Goodfellow Field San Angelo Texas
    Dear Mother, Jane, Wendy Ann and Dad,

I guess you are all together again after a swell vacation. That sure looked like an ideal spot. Boy could I go for some country like that after looking at the Texas desert. Things have been moving in typical army style after VJ. We did get two days off and a couple of us rented a cabin on a lake near Austin and just lay out in the sun and did a lot of swimming. We also rented a motor boat and putted around.

They immediately stopped primary training and started a new deal whereby you had to sign a statement that you were interested in the post war Air Force to continue training.

Well I didn't know what to do so instead of waiting around a couple of month for a discharge I decided to stay in and get as much flying time as possible and see how they discharge them.

You probably think I'm crazy to do a thing like this but if you had sat around waiting as much as I have, you'd understand. Don't worry if they ever mention anything like a three year hitch I'll resign so fast they won't even see my smoke. The way I look at it is that here is a chance to get some training that will be invaluable in years to come. If I did finish pilot training which will be in the spring of next year I could get a reserve commission with the right to fly army planes at the nearest army field. It is my desire to remain until the end of primary when I think they'll start discharging them. I will then resign and start bucking for my own discharge.

Well, I guess that's all the news.

Jack's War – Letters to home from an American WWII Navigator

Jack

134 – August 26th , 1945
Class 46-B Sqd 1
Goodfellow Field San Angelo Texas
    Dear Mother, Jane, Wendy Ann and Dad,

Had a very interesting week learning how to fly and have now got five hours in but as of Friday I'm washed up with the Army flying. They finally came out with a definite statement as to our status. To continue in training we had to sign up for the Post War Air Force and after graduating we would have to spend two years in the active reserve, probably with one year overseas as an occupational Air Force. Well you never know how close I came to signing up, but I didn't, and the latest is that we'll be at the Separation Centers for our discharge within two months. I wouldn't count on it knowing the Army as I do, and undoubtedly I will be the last to get out, for they will surely lose my papers or mess it up some way. It is going to be a slow death just to sit around here and wait, but I guess there is nothing I can do about it.

The flying was loads of fun, and I took to it like a duck to water and never had any trouble. Well, I guess that's all the news.

Jack

135 – August 28th , 1945
Class 46-B Sqd 1
Goodfellow Field San Angelo Texas
    Dear Mother, Jane, Wendy Ann and Dad,

Just a note to let you know what I'm doing. Sent to Washington D.C. yesterday for all my grades that I received in the Army so to be ready to go back to college and get as many credits as possible.

I'm trying to work out a deal while waiting down here to get a student's pilot license. I think I can solo in a couple of more hours of training so next week I may go out to the private field and buy two hours of training. If you remember I got ten hours of training in at Texas Tech which helps a lot. I need to have that log book which is either at home in my room or dad's study. I think Mother knows where it is. Please send it in a hurry for I need it as proof of my training. Well hope to see you in two months.

Jack

136 – September 2nd , 1945
Class 46-B Sqd 1
Goodfellow Field San Angelo Texas
    Dear Mother, Jane, Wendy Ann and Dad,

I guess my days in Texas are numbered but using a little army logic that I have garnered in the past two and a half years I doubt I will don civilian clothes in less than two months. I know this sounds incredible when they discharge them within a week of reporting to Santa Ana. I believe that the personal of "central training flying command" located at Randolph Field Texas has been affected by this Texas sun. I have signed no less than five different papers stating my preference for a discharge and each one has been ruled out because of some unofficial wording in the document. Until they can get an official one out my name I can't be sent into my representative separation center (Camp Beal). Now isn't that ridiculous but oh so typical of the Army Red Tape. I don't think I'll be able to do any flying for they have a new schedule to keep us busy, but I'm going to try anyway.

That sure is a cute picture of Wendy Ann, I can't wait to see her. Say when does the fall semester at Cal Aggies start? Oh yes, I got a notice that my bag from overseas was on its way home. Oh yes, my Plymouth has completely broken down and it will cost too much to fix it, so I'm going to sell it.

Jack's War – Letters to home from an American WWII Navigator

Well I'm just about out of news and questions.

Jack

137 – September 9th, 1945
Class 46-B Sqd 1
Goodfellow Field San Angelo Texas
Dear Mother, Jane, Wendy Ann and Dad,

Well another week and no news about our discharges. It really is amazing for all the "paddle feet" and "stateside commandos" are leaving the field every day for various separation centers, but that is the way it usually is. The permanent party takes care of themselves first, and then maybe help us if we've been real good. I guess you know I got on a three day cross country up to Omaha. We took off in an AT6 at 0900 Tuesday morning, stopped off in Enid Oklahoma for lunch and then landed at Omaha at 3:30 in the afternoon. We left Omaha Thursday at 2:00P.M. and gassed up at Enid and then flew to Sheppard Field, my first post, for dinner and then flew back that night and landed at !0:00 P.M.

Well that is all the news. I'm sure that log book is in my room somewhere. It is light brown in color.

Jack

138 – September 16th, 1945
Class 46-B Sqd 1
Goodfellow Field San Angelo Texas
Dear Mother, Jane, Wendy Ann and Dad,

Another week and no news as to my discharge. A lot of the Separation Centers have sent for the boys in my barracks but Camp Beale hasn't answered yet but I suspect they will within the next two weeks.

216

Boy that sure sounds like a swell trip Mother is going to take. I'd like to see the New England states myself. I don't see how you talked Mother into going by airplane though. Speaking of airplanes, we now have a "Junior Birdman" in the Woolsey family for I soloed yesterday out at the civilian airport in a 90 Horsy Over Cub. I'm working toward my Private Pilot's License so I can take you all for a ride. It costs about $8 an hour, but I can't think of a better way to spend my money.

Well Hope to be home soon so get them on the ball up there at Camp Beale.

Jack

139 – September 23rd, 1945
Goodfellow Field
San Angelo Texas
Dear Jane, Wendy Ann and Dad,

How are you three holding up out now that Mother has gone? I guess you heard about the new Air Corps separation centers they just set up. Well as luck would have it I'll be sent to Mc Cleland Field when the time comes. My name had been sent to Camp Beale and I was just waiting on a notice from there telling me when to report when they cancelled the whole thing and now we go through the same thing again.

I went to Austin this weekend to see the University of Texas play Bergstrom Field in football. They aren't too good but it was fun to see a game again. We went dancing that night and drove back today.

That sure is swell Linn dropped in to visit. I sure hope I get to see him. I'm flying every now and then out at the civilian airport, and I'm getting along fine. I hope to get my private pilot's license by 1946 and then I can take you for a ride.

Jack's War – Letters to home from an American WWII Navigator

Jack

140 – October 1st, 1945
Goodfellow Field
San Angelo, Texas
Dear Jane, Wendy Ann and Dad,

Well a new month and I hope to be home by the end of it especially since college starts the 26th. I'm just waiting for Mc Cleland to send a quota and then I'm pretty sure to go for I'm about third highest in points.

We're having quite a rain down here for a cold front moved in here Saturday morning. I had a little personal experience with it. I was out flying and took a little sightseeing trip when I got back to the field the edge of the storm was right at the edge of the field and the wind shifted 180° and became very gusty tossing me around like a cork. They motioned me not to land so I raced over to Goodfellow Field and tried to land there but the storm got there just ahead of me and so I started south to keep ahead of the storm and try to spot a field to land in. I located one of the army auxiliary fields and set it down just on front of the storm. I had to hold the plane down while the storm passed over and then I called back to the civilian field and told them where I was so they came over a got me.

That sure is swell that Linn is stationed in Suisun. I hope I get to see him. Mother sounds like she is having a wonderful time. Well that's all for now.

Jack

Note from Jack's father:
October 5th 1945
Jack arrived at the back door and was greeted by Toots. He looks good to us. Wendy was frightened by Jane's and my shouting. Had been travelling all day and night to California.

And so end an interesting chapter

April 2-1943 to October 9th, 1945 in the life of an American Youth

John Homer Woolsey Jr.

Jack immediately on his arrival home from Texas

HEADQUARTERS
ARMY AIR FORCES CENTRAL FLYING TRAINING COMMAND
Office of the Commanding General

Randolph Field, Texas

Mr. John H. Woolsey
163 Bartlett Street
Woodland, California

Dear MISTER Woolsey,

    Now that you have at last cleared the Separation Center and have enjoyed the thrill of again wearing "civvies", permit me to take this final opportunity to express my personal appreciation for the service you performed while you were a member of the AAF Central Flying Training Command.

    Those of us who have been soldiers for many years are the first to commend our great army composed almost entirely of civilians such as yourself who made possible our great victories in Europe and in the Pacific. You unselfishly gave up your normal civilian careers and modes of living to take up the unfamiliar ways of war. I know that the going was far from easy; that there were many gruelling, thankless, routine tasks; that many of you repeatedly risked your lives in uncomplainingly and courageously performing dangerous missions. I know, too, that there have been many heartaches during this terrible war. But, through it all, despite every difficulty, you stuck to the performance of those tasks, and the job of winning final victory was accomplished.

    For this selfless devotion to duty, I wish to extend my personal appreciation and to commend you for a job well done.

    Please permit me personally and on the behalf of the entire Army Air Forces, to extend you every best wish for a successful continuation of your interrupted civilian life. Regardless of whether we go forward as civilians or as members of the military, we are all Americans -- and as such, we will continue towards the goal we all seek -- a lasting and continuing peace, so that we may pursue the American way of life which we fought to preserve.

    Happy landings!

Yours very sincerely,

R. G. BREENE
Major General, U.S.A.
Commanding.

Happy Landings

Part 2

Mission Statements and Maps

In the E.T.O

Lt. John Woolsey

My tour in the ETO as Navigator with Bomber Crew 5750 starting October 8, 1944 and ending February 22, 1945.

We flew a liberator, B24 in the 564th Squadron of the 389th Bomb Group of the 8th Air Force.

We were based near Norwich.

Jack's War – Letters to home from an American WWII Navigator

Mission #1

Date – October 8th, 1944

Target - Airplane Motor Factory- Kassel

Weather- CAVU- all the way

Pilot-Whittier, Porter B
Co-pilot-King, James N
Navigator–Woolsey, John H
Bomb-Garringan, Leo
R/O-Lorraine, Anthony J
Engineer-Phelps, Auburn
T.T.-Berger, Chester D
A.G.-Jennings, Donald
A.E. Landrum, Charles
<u>Mission Notes</u>

Being our first mission we were all a little eager but no one seemed the least nervous. Everything went very smooth and according to Hoyle until we hit the I.P. Then little black clouds began appearing over the target and pretty soon we were right in it. The flak began to slam against the ship. After getting to the rally point Lorraine was covered with hydraulic fluid when he was going to shut the bomb bay doors. Our hydraulic system was shot up, so on reaching England we aborted and went to Woodbridge so as to make a safe landing. Due to low fog we homed in on Gee which is very reliable.

It was in the papers the next day that the flak was the heaviest ever experience in the E.T. O. I doubt this applied to our particular mission but I do know the flak was damn accurate.

Mission #1 Airplane Motor Factory- Kassel

Jack's War – Letters to home from an American WWII Navigator

Mission #2

Date – October 10th, 1944

Target -Marshalling Yards –Koblenz

Weather-under cast all the way

Crew- the same

<u>Mission Notes</u>

After our first baptism under fire I think we were all a little disappointed with this one. It was not run off too well, the course being changed half way across the Channel. Our primary target was a small airport just outside of Koblenz but due to the under cast we bombed Koblenz M.Y. by P.F. F. We saw some flak but none of it touched us. King thought he saw a buzz bomb and Berger relieved himself in his flak helmet. Outside of this it was a very dull mission.

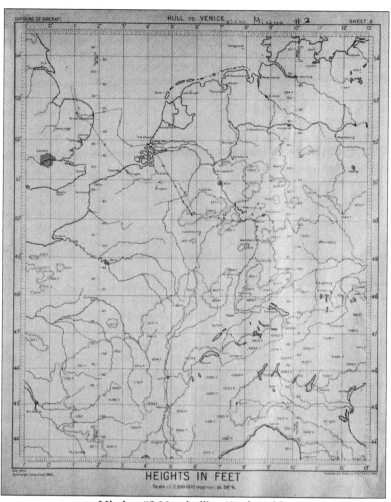

Mission #2 Marshalling Yards Koble

Mission #3

Date – October 17th, 1944

Target - Marshalling Yards – Cologne

Weather- Under Cast all the way

Crew- Same

Mission notes

After a week of idleness we were routed out of bed at 0330 and took off in the dark. After forming above the clouds we took off for Germany. Primary target was the oil storage tanks just outside of Cologne but due to the under cast we bombed the Marshalling yards P.F.F. Flak was off to our left and didn't touch us. We tried the new formation of six ships over the target with some success. This was just another repeat of Mission #2.

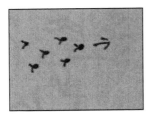

New Flying formation

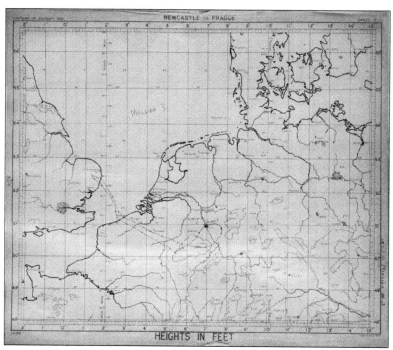
Mission #3 Marshalling Yards Cologne

Jack's War – Letters to home from an American WWII Navigator

Mission #4

Date – October 18th, 1944

Target-Farben Chemical Works-Cologne

Weather- Partially overcast

Crew- Same

Mission Notes

After getting the squadron officers pretty mad at us, King and I finally got us alerted for this mission. This was rather a special mission for FARBEN c. w. <u>was </u>(we hope) manufacturing poison gas and they sent out about 12 of us to wipe it out. The Jerries seemed to be prepared for us today for they really laid their flak right in there (six flak holes). Over the target they put it all around us and knocked out our #2 generator and supercharger which caused us to abort near the French Coast and cross the channel alone (Gee worked fine and came right in). Got a good look at the Rheine River and Koblenz also Brussels and Antwerp. Navigation was fair but due to high winds (100 mph) were a little off.

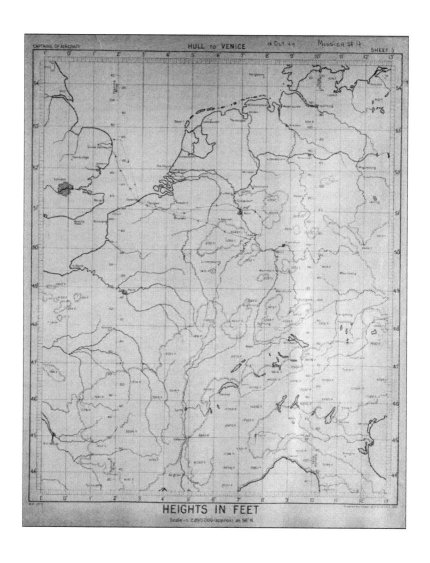

Mission #4 Farben Chemical works Cologne

Jack's War – Letters to home from an American WWII Navigator

Mission # 5

Date – October 22nd, 1944

Target - Marshalling Yards - Hamm

Weather - Overcast

Crew - same

Mission Notes

Seems as though the Germans patched up the last job we did and were sending reinforcements up to the western front so back we went today. Trip was uneventful following the briefed route and bombing P.F. F. Flak all around us but not too close. One event did stand out in the crew's minds and that was when they asked me if we were out of Germany and I assured them we were safely over German Lines and with that some battery opened up on us. I had some explaining to do on the account of the German held land just this side of the Zuider Zee. Crew working smoothly.

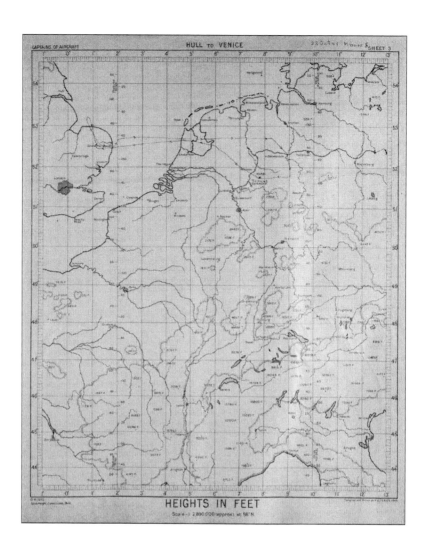

Mission #5 Marshalling Yards Hamm

Jack's War – Letters to home from an American WWII Navigator

Mission #6

Date – October 26th, 1944

Target – Marshalling Yards Munster

Weather - Overcast

Crew – Same

<u>Mission Notes</u>

After sweating out the weather for a couple of days, we finally got alerted for our Air Medical Mission. The missions are starting out later due to the late sunrise, but this leaves us more time in the sack so we don't mind. Well after a normal battle over Buncher six we lined out and were going right down the "chalk line" until we got over Germany. We were given the code word "Mae West" which meant we were bombing by G.H. on the primary target over Essen, but half way down the run they changed their minds and decided to bomb Munster P.F.F. Well they had to change lead planes, which is rather simple but dear old Capt. Schott and the P.F.F. lead managed to screw things up and had us spread out over Germany in two minutes. This could have proven fatal if there were any bandits in the area but we finally got lined out and dropped (we salvo-ed the bombs due to an intervalometer malfunction) our bombs in the vicinity of Munster. This was really a poor mission and shows the necessity of teamwork in the air. It also kind of bears out King's and my opinion (I don't know what to tell they guy, they should have left him pumping gas in the States.)

Gee was extra good today and picked up a fix (52-07N 06-33W) Tom Barrett more or less summed up the mission in one statement when he said "Tour de Ruhr with the 389th"

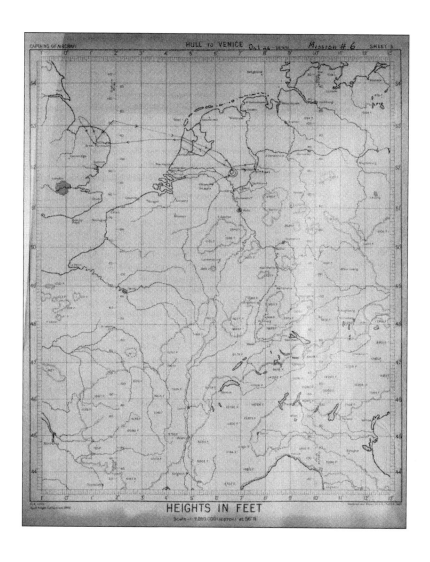

Mission #6 Marshalling Yards Munster

Jack's War – Letters to home from an American WWII Navigator

Mission #7

Date – November 2nd, 1944

Target – Train Trestle leading into Bielefeld

Weather - Partially under cast

Crew – Same

<u>Mission Notes</u>

After sweating out some bad weather and a 48 hr. pass we got our first Nov. mission in and it went all according to Hoyle. Saw quite a bit of Germany due to good weather and also saw our bombs hit the target not to mention the outskirts of Bielefeld and homes surrounding the train trestle. We knocked this trestle out so as to cut off the supplies being sent down to the Ruhr area. Flak was inaccurate and meagre but it is getting so you expect it anywhere in Germany. We even picked up some on the west side of the Zuider Zee. We haven't seen any German jet propelled yet but heard they knocked down two of our fighters.

Mission #8 Train Trestle leading to Bielefeld

Jack's War – Letters to home from an American WWII Navigator

Mission #8

Date – November 4th, 1944

Target – Synthetic Oil Plant- Gelsenkirchen

Weather - Partially under cast

Crew – Same

<u>Mission Notes</u>

Climbed to 18000 over Buncher 6, battled it out with several hundred planes and got off to and good start with "Happy Valley". After crossing the channel we had two props run away with us over Zuider Zee, but Whit and King got them under control quickly and we proceeded on with the temperature at about 35 below. When over the target in the Ruhr valley, flak covered the sky as predicted but didn't touch us. We dropped our bombs and got the hell out before it did. Nothing happened on the way back although Berger saw a German jet propelled playing tag with a couple of our P 47s and so ended mission #8.

Mission #8 Synthetic Oil Plant Gelsenkirchen

Jack's War – Letters to home from an American WWII Navigator

Mission #9

Date – November 5th, 1944

Target – Marshalling Yards- Karlsruhe

Weather - 8/10 under cast

Crew – Same

<u>Mission Notes</u>

We no sooner hit the sack then Whit said get up briefing at 5:00. This mission was a new one for us for we hadn't been down in the north-eastern France section before. We were briefed to hit some German defence fortifications which were giving our ground troops quite a bit of trouble around Metz. We carried 3-2000lb bombs which will blow anything to hell. Due to the cloud coverage we had to hit the secondary target Karlsruhe instead. This was the longest mission we'd been on lasting 7 ½ hours and the whole crew had a heck of a time keeping our eyes open when coming back across the channel. The flak at the target was intense but we just paid up our dues in the "Lucky Bastard" Club and it didn't even touch us except for one hole in the stabilizer. This flying every day is the berries and we hope the weather permits more of it.

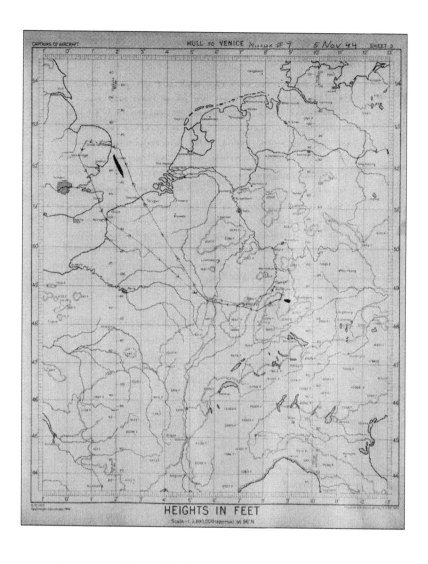

Mission #9 Marshalling Yards Karlsruhe

Jack's War – Letters to home from an American WWII Navigator

Mission #10

Date – November 9th, 1944

Target – Aines Fortification Metz

Weather – partially under cast

Crew – Same

Mission Notes

We were routed out of bed at 4:00 not knowing this would probably be one of the most strategically important missions of our tour. This was an all-out attempt to knock out the German Fortifications around Metz so General Patton's army which was stalled could make a break thru. We were very thoroughly briefed for it is a very ticklish job bombing two miles ahead of our troops with 3-2000lb bombs. Each plane was equipped with a special radio compass to determine the bomb line and also our own troops through up a line of flak 2000' below us so as to make sure we made no mistakes. Well we lined out and everything went well except our #4 engine was throwing a lot of oil and not drawing much power. The weather was under cast most of the way and it looked like we would have to bomb GH but there was a break just at the target and we really laid them in there. No flak was encountered but we had to feather #4 and abort the rally point and come back alone. I picked up a Gee fix about 3' E, determined our position and came in without any trouble. We almost landed in France but Whit decided we could make it and we did even though we did land in a hail storm. Right now we are just a little bit more than happy with the mission for we have received radio reports that "Blood and Guts" has broken through.

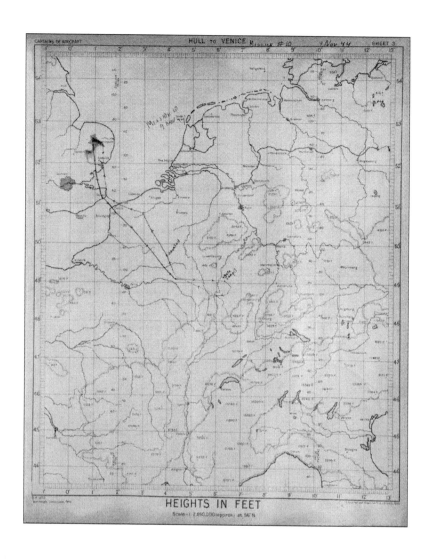

Mission #10 Aines Fortification Metz

Jack's War – Letters to home from an American WWII Navigator

Mission #11

Date – November 10th, 1944

Target – Hanau Airport 10 miles east of Frankfort

Weather – partially under cast GH

Crew – Same

<u>Mission Notes</u>

No sooner asleep than time to get up and chow up. It seems as though we are having a maximum effort while the good weather lasts. Today's target was a fighter base; the aim to disable it so Germany's fighters couldn't operate against our ground troops starting to move up towards this area. I might add that practically all of Germany's Luftwaffe is being used to aid their ground troops and that is why we are knocking out their airfields. We got lined out after forming south of London and everything went according to Hoyle except one bombardier salvo-ed his bombs by mistake and almost hit a ship. We went right into the target without any opposition and came back the same way except that we went over the edges of Koblenz by mistake and they almost knocked a couple of our ships out of the air. It was pretty cold at 24000'at -40 degrees and Germany had a blanket of snow over it. This was a 7 hr. mission so get ready sack, here I come.

Mission #11 Hanau Airport 10 miles east of Frankfort

Jack's War – Letters to home from an American WWII Navigator

Mission #12

Date – November 21st, 1944

Target – Synthetic Oil Plant - Hamburg

Weather – partially under cast

Crew – Same

<u>Mission Notes</u>

After knocking around on the ground for over a week and we drew a good one in Hamburg. We had an unfortunate accident while forming over the Bunches. Two of our planes collided sheering the wing off one and causing both to spin. It was a rather ghastly sight to see two large planes spiralling towards earth and no parachutes opening, although 3 did finally get out. Well this trip was rather a new one for it was mostly over water. When approaching the land near Wilhelmshaven they threw a smoke screen up but it didn't bother us. We went right on into Hamburg and they really must have had the Master Sergeants on duty for they threw up a hell of a barrage and had our altitude down to an inch, but we just walked on through and let them go right over the target. They tracked us right on through but couldn't seem to touch our plane although they did knock one of ours out. We made it back all right and enjoyed our northern tour of the Reich very much.

244

Mission #12 Synthetic Oil Plant Hamburg

Mission #13

t. Date – December 2nd, 1944

Target – Marshalling Yards Binger

Weather –under cast GH

Crew – Same

<u>Mission Notes</u>

We were just getting restless as hell just lying around and after being scrubbed twice we finally picked up a winner. After chowing up and briefing we finally took off. Oh yes the reason for hitting this target along the Rheine River was to stop the supplies into the Germans who were slowing down Patton's drive. Everything went fine and we just skimmed over the clouds and dropped our bombs with only four bursts of flak. We were just remarking what a milk run it was when bang, Jerry fighters streaked out of the clouds and knocked down two B24s one of which was in our low left section. Our gunners could see the 20mm bursting and also three parachutes come out of one of the ships. They didn't attack us but we all held our breath and waited. Well we got back all right but it was a grim reminder that we've got some tough ones ahead and the German Luftwaffe is not beaten by a long shot.

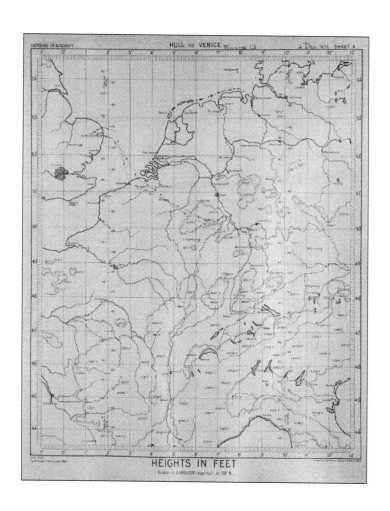

Mission #13 Marshalling Yards Binger

Jack's War – Letters to home from an American WWII Navigator

Mission #14

Date – December 4th, 1944

Target – Marshalling Yards Bebra

Weather –partially under cast

Crew – Same

Mission Notes

After some fast talking to Captain Kerns down at Operations we managed to get on the alert list. We assembled at 17500 and took off for Germany with a 100 knot wind at our backs. We were in the high right and had to keep S turning so as not to take over the lead. We were supposed to bomb GH but the signals faded and we dropped on the smoke bombs of the lead group. There was only one burst of flak and we started on the long trek back with our ground speed around 120 when we passed over Brussels. Phelps checked the gas and found we only had 250 gallons left. Rather than risk the chance of ditching in the channel we did a 180' and landed in Brussels Melsbroek A.F. and spent the night in Brussels. Whit spent the night guarding the plane while we all went in and looked the town over. We took off the next morning after loading up with gas and landed at Hethel at 12:00. A very successful mission.

Mission #14 Marshalling Yards Bebra

Jack's War – Letters to home from an American WWII Navigator

Mission #15

Date – December 12th, 1944

Target – Maximilian Scow Rail Road Bridge Karlsruhe

Weather –under cast GH

Crew – Same

<u>Mission Notes</u>

After routing out the entire field for this mission we took off and formed at 10000 feet. Knocking out this bridge was a direct request from the ground forces so as to reduce their supply lines into the Strasbourg battle area. They jumped up the zero hour and we had to cut a couple of corners, but this didn't bother us. We got there without any trouble and Whit and King handled their first section lead dam good. The flak was meagre and inaccurate although a couple of wild pieces slapped the side of our ship. I had a 27 RF unit and got Gee fixes all the way into the target. We got back okay and on the whole it was a very dull mission.

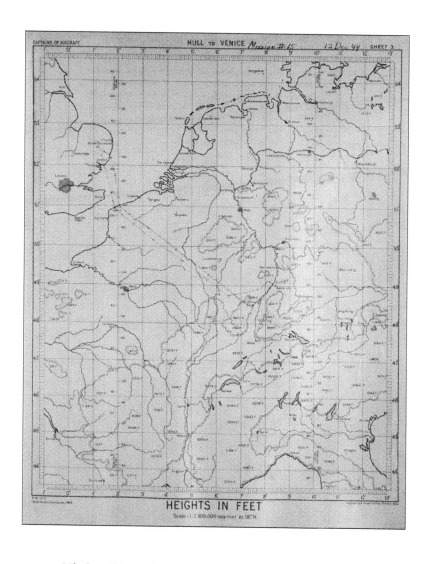

Mission #15 Maximilian Scow RR Bridge Karlsruhe

Jack's War – Letters to home from an American WWII Navigator

Mission #16

Date – December 19th, 1944

Target – Marshalling Yards Trier

Weather –under cast

Crew – Same

Mission Notes

After being scrubbed in the briefing room, out at the plane and over Belgium forced us to take to the air in the "London Fog" and I might add Whit and King gave us quite a thrill on the take off by dam near going off the runway. We went over and bombed without anything unusual occurring and got back to the coast without a scratch, but while crossing we got word that the base was socked in so we went to the alternative base in southern England "St Mawgan" and stayed there four days before being able to return. It is the general concern that the Germans timed their counter attack with the weather and did a good job of it.

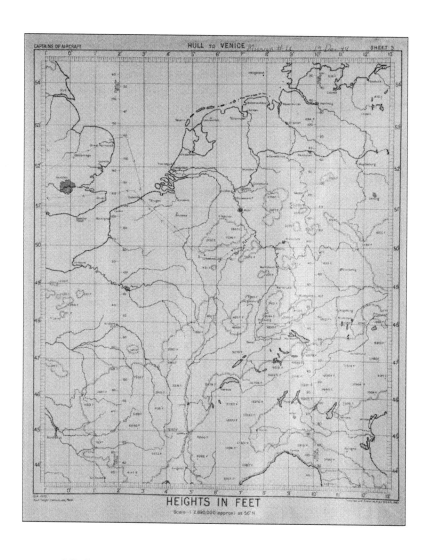

Mission #16 Marshalling Yards Trier

Jack's War – Letters to home from an American WWII Navigator

Mission #17

Date – December 24th, 1944

Target – Marshalling Yards -Born

Weather –CAVU

Crew – Same

<u>Mission Notes</u>

After coming back from "St Mawgan" we brought the good weather with us; the 8th set a record by putting up everybody and his dog and we really had a field day over the Reich delivering Christmas packages in the form of 12- 500 lbs. It was clear as a bell and we bombed visual. We were in the slot of the high right and when we came to the Primary which the lead demolished. The lead's bomb racks had a malfunction and did not release so we sailed over and then picked up the Marshalling Yards as a military target and bombed the hell out of it as well as the surrounding town. We got in some flak today and it was too darn close for our money. We heard that old familiar "Whoomp Whoomp" and it really rocked us but old lady luck was right up there and although it tore a few holes in our ship, it didn't hit any of us or vital parts of the plane. We came right home and were greeted by Captain Cowboy Kern, and he gave us glad tidings that weather permitting we could play Santa Claus to the Jerries again tomorrow.

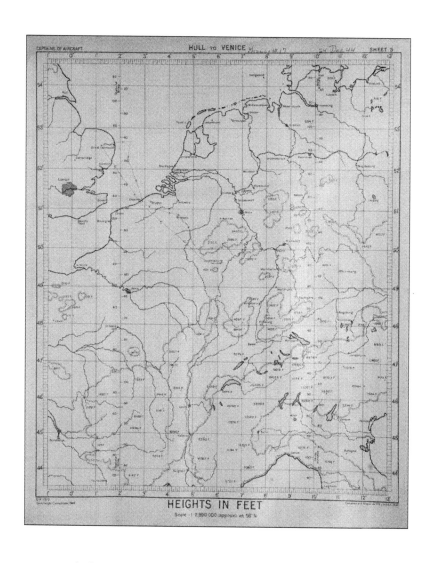

Mission # 17 Marshalling Yards -Born

Jack's War – Letters to home from an American WWII Navigator

Mission #18

Date – December 25th, 1944

Target – Wahlen

Weather –CAVU

Crew – Same

Mission Notes

We were awakened 0430 on the lovely Christmas morning, but it wasn't for unwrapping our Christmas presents. It was to deliver some to the Germans and what a field day the Air Corps had. When we got over the target area the whole territory was on fire. There were fighters on the deck strafing the roads and hundreds of Bomber blowing up different towns. We didn't have too rough of a bomb run, but did pick up a couple of flak holes after we dropped our bombs the right got jumped by fighters and before they left they knocked down three of our planes, one blowing up and crashing. The target was just a small town behind the lines but it is an all-out effort to blow everything up behind the lines so as to stop the German counter offensive.

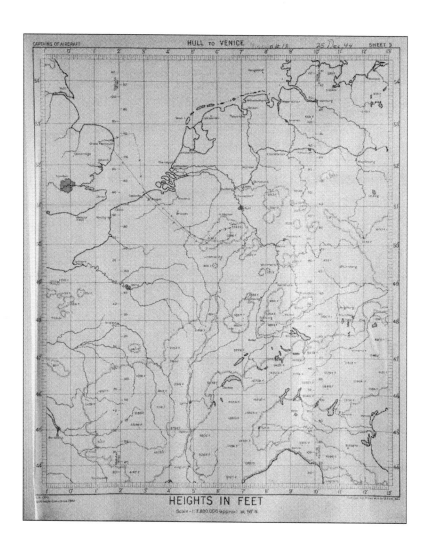

Mission # 18 Whalen

Jack's War – Letters to home from an American WWII Navigator

Mission #19

Date –December 27th, 1944

Target – Marshalling Yards- Kaiserslautern

Weather –CAVU

Crew – Same

<u>Mission Notes</u>

With the "high" still sitting over the continent and the weather colder than hell on our own base, we donned our "long johns" and started another one. While forming over the buncher Jennings and Berger took off the waist window to clean the frost off and while doing so the wind whipped it out of their hands and it few back and gashed our tail but we went anyway. The trip was uneventful up to the target where we got a burst of flak in the front of the #3 engine, one piece coming through the side and landing against King's heel, but the side of the ship stopped the force and he was uninjured. We returned and could not land at our base due to the fog so we landed at Hardwick and came back by truck.

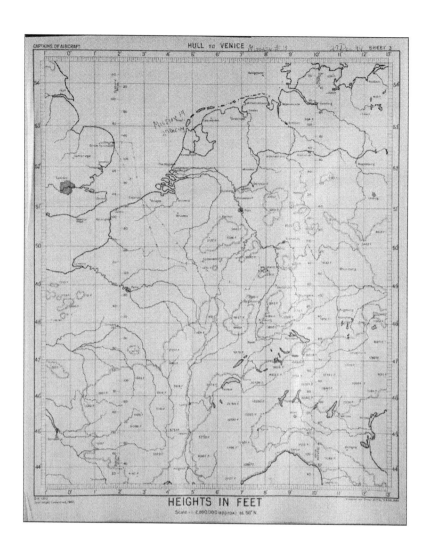

Mission # 19 Marshalling Yards- Kaiserslautern

Jack's War – Letters to home from an American WWII Navigator

Mission #20

Date –December 29th, 1944

Target – Born-Born (Target of opportunity)

Weather –Partially under cast

Crew – Same

<u>Mission Notes</u>

Just another one of our all our efforts to tie up Van Rundstedt offensive by bombing every town and railway junction near lines. One might wonder why we are bombing some of these small towns off the map and what effect it would have on stopping the German drive. Right now these towns are loaded with supplies and troops where before they were just a small town. It was a very ordinary mission with small flak, but just as we were about to drop our bombs a group of B17s passed beneath us so we had to go on and find another target which we did and bombed it.

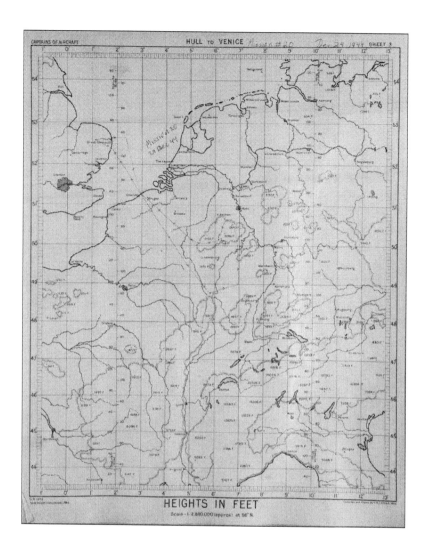

Mission #20 Born-Born (Target of opportunity)

Jack's War – Letters to home from an American WWII Navigator

Mission #21

Date – January 2nd, 1945

Target – Rail Road Bridge-Koblenz

Weather –8/10 under cast

Crew – Same (King now co-pilot flew with new crew)

<u>Mission Notes</u>

After spending a two day pass in Gt. Yarmouth, we struck our first 1945 blow for liberty. We came in the back door and had clean sailing right into the target except myself as I was having trouble keeping my breakfast down due to too many light ales New Year night. When we got over the Rail Road bridge leading into Koblenz we noticed that there was a particular scarcity of flak and were still remarking about 10 miles away from the target when all of a sudden little black puffs of smoke appeared right out on the wing tips and went "whoomp whoomp" and boy we were right in the midst of one of the most accurate barrages we've hit. I can't see why we weren't knocked down, but there were a couple of holes in the ship and everybody was safe and sound and that was it.

Mission #21 Rail Road Bridge-Koblenz

Jack's War – Letters to home from an American WWII Navigator

Mission #22

Date – January 3rd, 1945

Target – Marshalling Yards- Pirmasens

Weather –10/10 under cast

Crew – Same

<u>Mission Notes</u>

Possibly one of the most unexciting one of them all was our 22nd. We flew the High Right for the 445th and bombed the town through the clouds. We didn't see flak or have any trouble at all.

Mission #22 Marshalling Yards- Pirmasens

Mission #23

Date – January 5th, 1945

Target – Rail Road Junction Neunstedt

Weather –Partially under cast

Crew – Same

<u>Mission Notes</u>

With a front lying over Belgium and snow storms in our own area, we took off and formed over Sp 11 south of London and what a time we had. We went to 19500' and couldn't find the group, then we got a message over VHF that we were assembling at 15000 on account of the mist and con trails. We went down and still couldn't find them and it was time to start so we took off across the channel and finally found them about 30 miles out. We topped the front and sailed in without any opposition and got a visual run at the target. At bombs away they let go with an accurate barrage of flak and one whacked the front of our ship and a piece smacked us right on the nose glancing off the bomb sight but not touching Leo or me so we came home and chalked up #23.

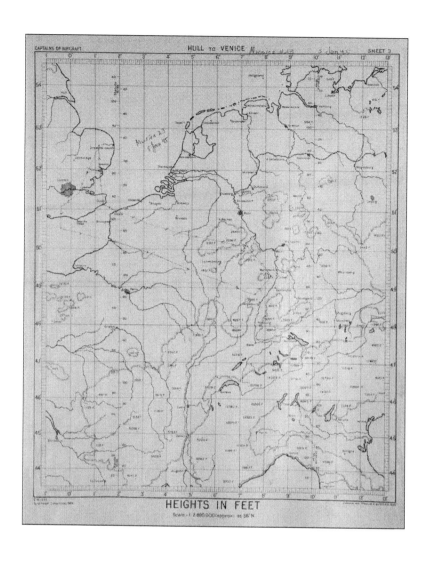

Mission #23 Rail Road Junction Neustadt

Jack's War – Letters to home from an American WWII Navigator

Mission #24

Date – January 6th, 1945

Target Bridge Bonn

Weather –8/10 under cast

Crew – Same

Mission Notes

Up for the 4th time in the last 5 days, we were a bit tired, but pretty eager to get our "3rd cluster" mission in. Had no trouble forming, but we saw a lot of V2 con trails on our way in. Mission went as briefed but dropped our bombs one at a time (1 electrically, 1 salvo-ed, and the other Leo had to crawl out and kick loose with a screw driver). This cold weather is freezing up the bomb mechanisms causing a lot of malfunctions. The flak was light and inaccurate. Returned home without incident.

Mission #24 Bridge Bonn

Jack's War – Letters to home from an American WWII Navigator

Mission #25

Date – January 10th, 1945

Target- Rail Road Junction St Vith

Weather –partially under cast

Crew – Same

Mission Notes

After sweating out the cold weather and one trip half way into France at 55 below, we drew a short one right on the Belgium border. We didn't fly our plane for King left it in France. It was sure cold 50 below and I had frost all over my eyebrows. We got over the target in no time, but had to make two runs before we released on G.H. We only saw two bursts of flak, but they must have been aiming for us for a piece just missed our two gunners and we also got a couple of big holes in the tail.

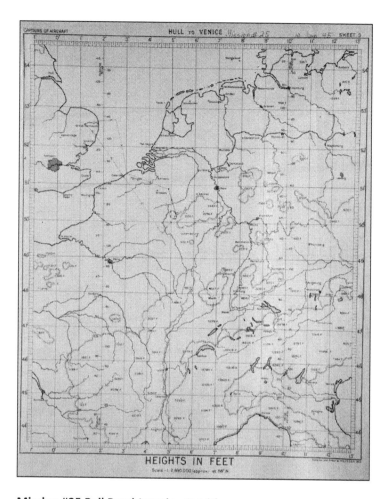

Mission #25 Rail Road Junction St Vith

Jack's War – Letters to home from an American WWII Navigator

Mission #26

Date – January 16th, 1945

Target- Krupp (Tanks) - Magdeburg

Weather –partially under cast

Crew – Same

<u>Mission Notes</u>

Our 26th was a veritable "Cooks Tour" of Germany, being used as fighter bait but to no avail. We got a late take off, but joined the low left as Deputy Lead and took off for the Reich. We were over clouds until about 8"E and then it broke and we got a wonderful view of the countryside and kept a weather eye out for fights and flak. There was a cloud bank over the target so we made a PFF run and when we straightened out of the bomb run we were headed for the secondary target instead of the Primary (Synthetic oil plant) so instead of turning on the bomb run, Major Tolleson decided to hit the secondary. There was little flak and we dropped and got out quick and when we looked back there was a wall of flak you could walk on. We headed south and came out the southern route. Our field was closed in so the High Right landed at Paris while the lead and the low left came back to Northern England and landed at a Canadian base and came back next morning.

GOING TO THE FLAK HOUSE!!!!

(R&R for Officers)

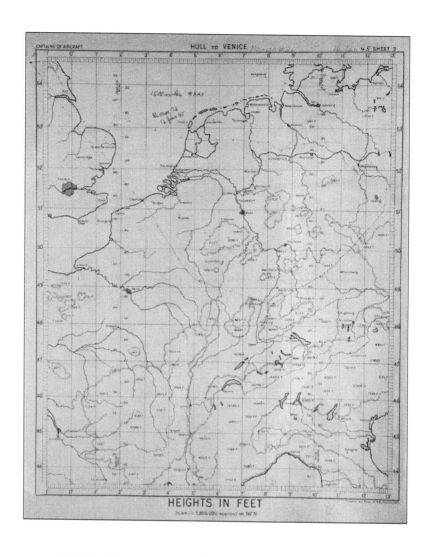

Mission # 26 Krupp (Tanks) Magdeburg

Jack's War – Letters to home from an American WWII Navigator

Mission #27

Date – January 29th, 1945

Target- Marshalling Yards - Hamm

Weather –partially under cast PFF

Crew – Same * J East as co-pilot

<u>Mission Notes</u>

After spending a swell 10 days at the "flak house" we were all pretty eager to get started again. We were briefed to hit a small Rail Road viaduct just northeast of Paderborn, but due to heavy cover we hit Hamm Marshalling Yards as a secondary. We were flying in the high right and failed to get more flak, but the low left caught hell and one more ship got a direct hit and blew up. The navigation was pretty poor and the Gee was all snafu. Lately we have seen the V2 bomb con trails rising from Germany.

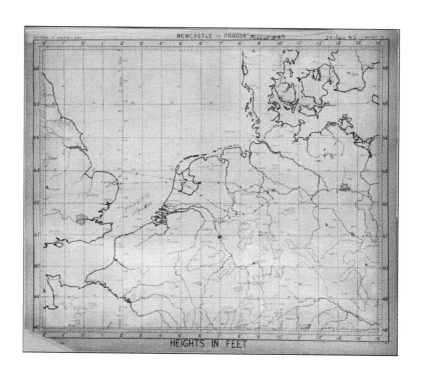

Mission # 27 Marshalling Yards - Hamm

Jack's War – Letters to home from an American WWII Navigator

Mission #28

Date – January 31st, 1945

Target- Goering Steel Works-Brunswick

Weather –10/10 under cast under cast PFF

Crew – Same

<u>Mission Notes</u>

With plan A to Berlin we drew plan B because of the weather and were sailing along when we got the recall word and turned around to come back. This was due to the fact the fighters didn't get off and the English bases were closing in. We didn't drop our bombs until over the English Channel and we all wondered why for we had several targets of opportunity but orders are orders and the reason we were given was some of the wings were over Holland and they didn't want anyone to drop on her. We had a hard time finding a clear base but finally set her down at Thornaby. One of the boys ran into a tree and killed all but the pilot. We came back the next day after spending the night in town.

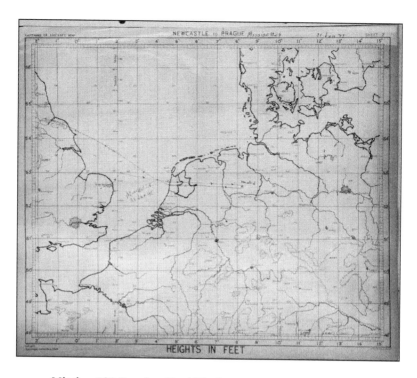

Mission #28 Goering Steel Works Brunswick

Jack's War – Letters to home from an American WWII Navigator

Mission #29

Date – February 6th, 1945

Target- Marshalling Yards - Magdeburg

Weather –partially under cast

Crew – Same

Mission Notes

After having Berlin and Munich scrubbed out from under us we finally got one in to Magdeburg. The 8th A.F. is starting to level these towns the way they should be and Boy! Are the Germans crying in their beer over our murderous tactics. What a joke after their V2 over London. We got formed ok but a fellow stalled out some prop wash and crashed with the bombs exploding (ball of fire rose a 1000'in the air). We climbed and crossed the Dutch coast and darned if one of those two gun batteries didn't blow a wing off some ship behind us. We sailed into the target on course and dropped PFF with very little flak to bother us and we returned without incident. So ends the 29th.

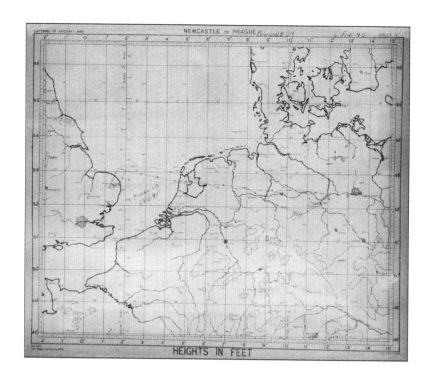

Mission # 29 Marshalling Yards - Magdeburg

Jack's War – Letters to home from an American WWII Navigator

Mission #30

- Date – February 9th, 1945

- Target- Viaduct -Bielefeld

- Weather –partially under cast

- Crew – Same

    o <u>Mission Notes</u>

    o This target is a regular customer of the 8th A.F. and nobody knows why or gives a dam for the flak is light and it is a short trip. We went in as briefed and came out without a scratch.

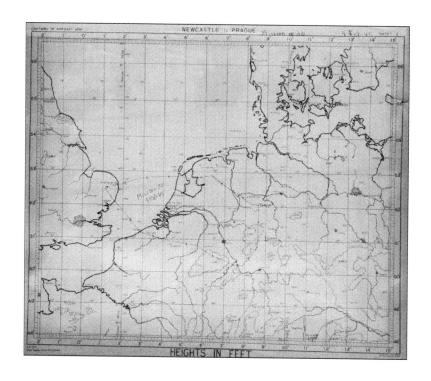

Mission 30 Viaduct -Bielefeld

Jack's War – Letters to home from an American WWII Navigator

Mission #31

Date – February 14th, 1945

Target- Marshalling Yards - Magdeburg

Weather –partially under cast

Crew – Same

Mission Notes

Flying under our new group set up (that is each squadron taking over one of the flight squadrons instead of mixing everyone together) we drew Magdeburg for the third time which isn't exactly advantageous to one's health. We got formed okay and flew a perfect briefed route in and the code word given to bomb the secondary instead of the Primary oil plant (about the only thing left standing in Magdeburg). We were in flak for quite a while but managed to stay clear except Phelps who got a piece of flak thru the top turret and just missed him. It put a big hole in the plexiglass, but didn't hurt anyone. We came out pretty slow due to the 80 mile headwind but we finally made it losing only one ship over the target.

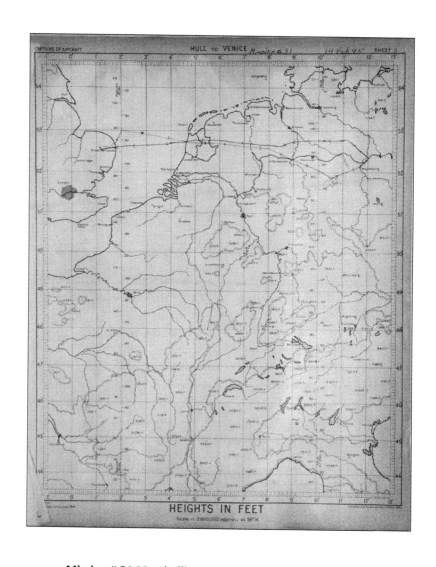

Mission # 31 Marshalling Yards - Magdeburg

Jack's War – Letters to home from an American WWII Navigator

Mission #32

Date – February 16th, 1945

Target- Marshalling Yards – Rheine

Weather –partially under cast

Crew – Same

<u>Mission Notes</u>

Determined to keep the attack on the Rail Road lines we took off in a pea soup fog and dropped over to Rheine to blast their Marshalling Yards. Flak was meagre and inaccurate. Two of our bombs got hung up and the two above them came down and jammed, tearing lose their arming wire and their propellers turning. This means they were armed and a slight push and they would go off. Leo did a good job and had them out in four minutes. The route back was uneventful but Whit and King did a nice job in landing in the fog-so ended 32.

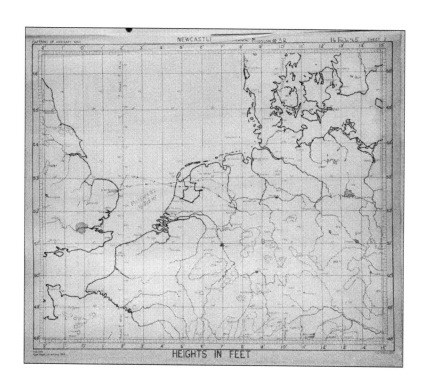

Mission #32 Marshalling Yards – Rheine

Jack's War – Letters to home from an American WWII Navigator

Mission #33

Date – February 19th, 1945

Target- Tiger Tank Factory-

Weather –partially under cast

Crew – Same

Mission Notes

Well, being pretty near the end we are all eager to finish up but we just can't seem to get excited about it. We flew deputy head of the low left and had a very orderly mission. We formed up with Lorraine firing red flares all over East Anglia. We were over clouds all the way into the target and dropped our bombs GH and broke away and didn't see a burst of flak except off to our right over Koblenz. We saw plenty of mediums going into blast their targets. We returned without incident and thus ends 33.

Mission #33 Tiger Tank Factory

Jack's War – Letters to home from an American WWII Navigator

Mission #34

Date – February 21st, 1945

Target- Marshalling Yards - Nurnberg

Weather –partially under cast

Crew – Same

<u>Mission Notes</u>

Plan A was to Berlin and everybody was sure we were really going but I guess we're destined never to hit Berlin for at the last minute we switched to plan B which was Nurnberg where the German High Command was supposed to have evacuated to, along with the Berlin flak guns. Well it was a beautiful day and we climbed on course and bombed the PFF with little flak opposition which was to our liking due to the fact we could see the ground most of the way. We really must have wiped the target off the map for the whole 8th A.F. blasted it: Well just one more.

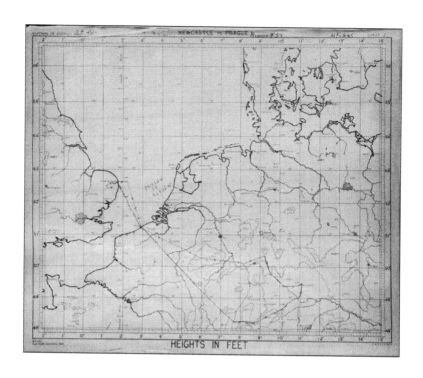

Mission #34 Marshalling Yards Nurnberg

Jack's War – Letters to home from an American WWII Navigator

Mission #35

Date – February 22nd, 1945

Target- Marshalling Yards - Sangerhausen

Weather –clear

Crew – Same

<u>Mission Notes</u>

Needless to say we were plenty eager to get our last one in and I can say without a doubt it was the most exciting one we were on. This was the 8th A.F. heaviest blow of the war and it was aimed at the Marshalling Yards all over Germany, to tie up their transportation between the Eastern and Western front. It was timed with the weather so as to have a clear day. A "high" rolled over Germany and left just a small amount of middle cloud and took a chance and this is where the 8th A.F. pulled an ace out of their sleeve. Due to the fact we had to do precision bombing they had us bomb at 10000' which hasn't been done by the big birds since Ploesti. Well we formed up and took off and climbed to 18000' over the Zuider Zee and then started to let down over Bielefeld and we really had to stay on course or the flak would have knocked the hell out of us. Boy it seemed we were really down on the deck when we reached 7000' and we saw what Germany looked like. The gunners started opening up on some of the small town Marshalling Yards, and they really made the dust fly. You could see their traces smack right into the buildings. The S2 really had the situation tabbed for the Marshalling Yards were really loaded. Coming up one of the valleys our hearts stood still for an un-plotted flak battery opened up and we were like sitting ducks at 7000'. We just knocked on wood and roared by. We dropped our bombs and blew the hell out of the target while our gunners kept on strafing. We felt the explosion of the bombs but got away ok. Two FW 190 were down on deck but didn't dare come up to tackle us due to the good fighter support. It was really an experience down there but boy it makes you sweat. We got back in fine shape and when we came over the field the two other crews finishing up got in formation and we gave them a buzz job they won't forget. Johnson was about 6 ' off the runway with King socked in tighter than a drum and going 250 mph. Boy we really roared down the runway and gave them a thrill. Well we landed and went into briefing which was full of war correspondents getting the dope on our record Bombing Mission. We were all congratulated for finishing up and thus ended a very successful tour in the E.T. O.

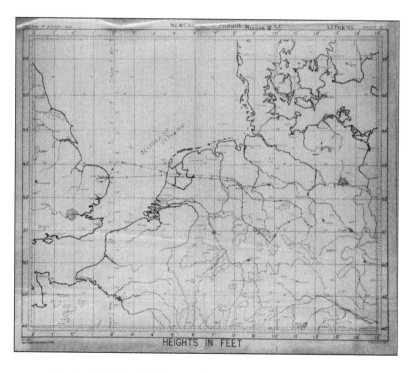

Mission #35 Marshalling Yards Sangerhausen

Epilogue

As with many men, Jack was late in getting discharged and resuming his college career. His close college friend, Peter Kennedy, had started veterinary school at Kansas State a month earlier after his own discharge from the Army Air Corps.

Peter went to the Dean of the veterinary school and asked if he would consider letting Jack join the class. The dean asked if Jack was a good student.

"Not particularly" replied Peter honestly.

The Dean asked if Jack was smart, good with animals or experienced with veterinary medicine.

Peter admitted his friend did not excel or have experience in veterinary medicine.

Finally, the Dean asked if Jack was good looking.

Peter smiled and replied an emphatic "yes".

"Okay, tell him to get here right away."

Jack Woolsey got into veterinary school based on his good looks and graduated with Peter from Kansas State in 1949 and went on to have a long happy career in veterinary medicine in Sonoma County, California. He was married and had five children, imported and raised Kelpies, but his real passion was horses and thoroughbred racing. He died in 2011.

Elizabeth Woolsey Herbert DVM

Elizabeth grew up in post war California. She followed in her father's footsteps into equine veterinary practice and worked for her father until his retirement. She subsequently migrated to Australia where she practices veterinary medicine at Adelaide Plains Equine Clinic outside Adelaide, South Australia.

She began writing about her experiences as a horse vet, and published her first book

Horse Doctor An American Vet's Life Down Under in 2005.

Her father rarely talked about his war experiences, and their bond through veterinary medicine, philosophy and horses was the basis of their relationship. When a few years before his death she discovered this treasure trove of both personal and historically significant communication, she knew this was going to make a great book not only for her family, but also for WWII enthusiasts.

While veterinary medicine is her passion, fly fishing, horseback riding and writing occupy her leisure time.

Contact info:
Elizabeth Woolsey Herbert DVM
1951 Two Wells Rd
Gawler 5118
Australia
ewhdvm@internode.on.net
+61 885234777
Or find her on Facebook

Jack's War – Letters to home from an American WWII Navigator

Made in the USA
San Bernardino, CA
04 May 2016